The Feeling of Transcendence, an Experience of God?

The Feeling of Transcendence, an Experience of God?

LOUIS ROY

WIPF & STOCK · Eugene, Oregon

THE FEELING OF TRANSCENDENCE, AN EXPERIENCE OF GOD?

Copyright © 2021 Louis Roy. All rights reserved. Except for brief quotations in critical publications or reviews, no part of this book may be reproduced in any manner without prior written permission from the publisher. Write: Permissions, Wipf and Stock Publishers, 199 W. 8th Ave., Suite 3, Eugene, OR 97401.

Wipf & Stock
An Imprint of Wipf and Stock Publishers
199 W. 8th Ave., Suite 3
Eugene, OR 97401

www.wipfandstock.com

PAPERBACK ISBN: 978-1-7252-7274-3
HARDCOVER ISBN: 978-1-7252-7273-6
EBOOK ISBN: 978-1-7252-7275-0

03/12/21

The Scripture quotations contained herein are from the New Revised Standard Version of the Bible, copyrighted 1989 by the Division of Christian Education of the National Council of the Churches of Christ in the United States of America, and are used by permission. All rights reserved.

Contents

Preface | vii
Introduction | ix

1 **The Feeling of What Transcends Us** | 1
   Three Accounts | 1
   Affinities and Differences | 10

2 **Slow-Motion Replay** | 15
   Constitutive Elements | 16
   A Classic Text | 23

3 **Families of Mindsets** | 27
   Examples | 29
   A Case of Aesthetic Experience | 34
   A Case of Ontological Experience | 35
   A Case of Ethical Experience | 39
   A Case of Interpersonal Experience | 42

4 **Rejections** | 46
   Ludwig Feuerbach | 47
   Sigmund Freud | 53

5 **A Prophetic Denunciation?** | 59
   Historical Considerations | 61
   A First Set of Writings | 62
   A Later Contribution | 65
   A Suspicion in Need of Interpretation | 67

6 Critiques | 70
   From Rejection to Critique | 70
   The Oceanic Feeling | 74
   The Mother's or Father's Religion? | 77

7 Validation | 82
   Intentionality and the Holy Spirit | 82
   The Psyche and the Road to Maturity | 84
   Self-awareness and Otherness | 86
   Evil and the Non-experience of God | 91
   The Role of Spiritual Guides | 94

8 The Transcendent Experience and Jesus Christ | 97
   Is There a Correct Interpretation? | 98
   An Interpretive Approach | 99
   The Challenge of a Personalist Interpretation | 100
   A Question of Credibility | 102

Conclusion | 103
Bibliography | 107

Preface

For those living in these early decades of the twenty-first century, consciousness is pervaded by a sense of disillusionment. Life is difficult for countless people: unemployment, lack of job security, collective debt (except in well-to-do nations), violence, in some cases irreversible damage to the environment, the loss of warmth in soulless societies. Amid this grim landscape, where hope struggles against indifference, many are searching for somewhere that is more colorful and richer. This explains people's interest in sects, Gnosticism, esotericism, spirituality, meditation, and Zen.

We are justified in asking whether this keen interest in interiority reflects a desire to escape reality. We would have to be blind to avoid noticing some kind of attempt to compensate for the disappointments caused by workplaces and politics. That being said, the fact remains that questions about the spiritual are an essential part of human development. As I present my thoughts on the feeling of transcendence, I wish to share the following belief: transcendent experiences can be healthy—in fact, they are a source of significant personal growth for those who recognize them and allow themselves to be challenged by them. Once they have been spiritually renewed, those who have been awakened by such experiences, whether they are rich, poor, or middle class, are often better equipped to carry out their social responsibilities.

The aim of this book is therefore to help readers to situate their transcendent experiences within the broader framework

Preface

of human existence, to tap into the astonishing potential within them, and to become mystics, in joy, suffering, and perseverance. The approach will be ecumenical, since this can foster an encounter among spiritualities and religions. I will focus on that which unites rather than that which divides. As I discuss the matter of criteria of discernment, my objective will be to provide guidance in the search for authenticity. Finally, especially in the last chapter, I will make a link to Christianity, whose strength lies not in condemning, but in lifting up, purifying, and integrating.

For more than twenty-five years, the accounts of transcendent experiences that I have collected have been discussed in classes I have taught in Boston and Montreal. I wish to thank all the students who shared their views as I presented my theories on the subject and who helped me to clarify or revise these theories. Friends have also offered very useful suggestions regarding the style and clarity of my writing, as well as different ways to more fully incorporate readers' concerns into the text.

I would like to thank Pierre LaViolette and Anne Louise Mahoney for having translated and edited this book, which was originally published in French under the title *Le Sentiment de transcendence, expérience de Dieu* ? (Paris: Cerf, 2000). Chapter 8 is an addition to the French edition.

Introduction

Whether within their ordinary lives or within churches and religious groups, people of all ages and of various social backgrounds report having had unique experiences that are rooted in a feeling of transcendence, which they interpret in various ways.

Such experiences have been documented. A 1973 survey conducted in the United States by William McCready and Andrew Greeley revealed that millions of people—35 percent of the country's population—admitted having had contact with a spiritual power that seemed to lift them above themselves.[1] A 1964 *Newsweek* survey showed a similar result: 33 percent of Americans surveyed reported having had a religious experience of a mystical nature. Furthermore, the same survey indicated that 68 percent of respondents said they had experienced a sense of the sacred during the birth of a child.

In England, zoologist-philosopher Sir Alister Hardy and his team from Manchester College, Oxford, studied the subject in depth.[2] In the wake of Hardy's work, David Hay searched at length for the best question to use in a survey. He finally settled on the following: "Have you ever been aware of or influenced by a presence or power, whether you call it God or not, which is different from your everyday self?" This question was used in a survey by

---

1. See Greeley, *Sociology of the Paranormal*, 57–58. Other interesting correlations are found in chapter 4.

2. See Hardy, *Spiritual Nature*. The center was originally called the Religious Experience Research Unit, but was renamed the Alister Hardy Religious Experience Research Centre following the death of its founder.

Introduction

National Opinion Polls in Great Britain. In a country where Sunday church attendance is significantly lower than that of the United States, the percentage of 'yes' answers was similar (36 percent; 31 percent according to another survey). Interestingly, about 25 percent of agnostics and atheists answered 'yes' to this question.[3]

Similar results have been obtained in Canada. In surveys conducted from 1975 to 2000 by sociologist Reginald Bibby, nearly half of Canadians (just under 50 percent) reported having had a "feeling that you have experienced God's presence."[4] Bibby adds: "Older Canadians are only marginally more inclined than their younger counterparts to claim they have had such an experience."[5] In a separate publication dealing specifically with teens, he reports a similar level of positive response: approximately 4 in 10 (36 percent) believe they have "felt [the] presence of God/a higher power."[6]

The results of such surveys require careful interpretation. Everything depends on how we define the perceived experience. When it is described in religious terms, the results are high among people who attend church regularly.[7] However, when it is couched in secular terms, without being presented as life-changing or extraordinary, many people who keep their distance from churches admit to having had such experiences.[8]

During the 1970s, something comparable happened among the intelligentsia of the completely secularized Soviet Union. In a Russian publication that was translated and published in French, a witness states: "People who approach the Church today have no religious experience whatsoever, no hint of personal affinity or

---

3. See Hay, *Exploring Inner Space*, 116–34. These pages present many other interesting statistics and correlations.

4. Bibby, *Restless Gods*, 146.

5. Bibby, *Restless Gods*, 150.

6. Bibby, *Canada's Teens*, 123.

7. For example, the Glock and Stark study, done in California in 1965, which found that between 66 percent and 73 percent of Christians stated that they had had a feeling of the presence of God. See Hay, *Exploring Inner Space*, 120.

8. See Hay, *Exploring Inner Space*, 166.

Introduction

intact childhood memories. . . . For the present generation, there is no use trying to find traces of the Church within their memory."[9] He adds: "I am speaking from experience: people who grew up outside of organized religious life woke up one day as committed Christians—not weekday mass attendees, but ardent neophytes whose passion may disturb those around them."[10] He later explains that in the ideological void of those years, artists, scientists, and technicians sensed "the feeling of another reality, the pull of the Word of God."[11]

What about the rest of Europe? Unfortunately, I was unable to find any statistics. However, the feeling of transcendence is found in many passages in German, English, and French literature: for example, in Goethe, Wordsworth, Chateaubriand, and Proust. For the purposes of this book, I will examine the French writers Romain Rolland, Jean-Paul Sartre, Julien Green, Simone Weil, Jacques Maritain, and Madeleine Delbrêl, as well as German thinkers such as Kant, Schleiermacher, Otto, Heidegger, Karlfried Graf von Dürckheim (a psychiatrist, not to be confused with the French sociologist Émile Durkheim), Tillich, Fromm, and Berger, all of whom touch on this transcendent experience.

A look back at the past reveals an inexhaustible source of information on transcendent experience in the Bible, in the history of religions, and in the world of mysticism.[12] Poets, novelists, philosophers, psychologists, and scientists attest to this experience. Most of the data I will use is both simple and modern. Simple because I want to focus on people's and groups' initial openness to the transcendent, instead of the later stages of the spiritual

---

9. Zielinski, "Une nouvelle génération," 71; see 69–123.

10. Zielinski, "Une nouvelle génération," 72. This phenomenon is confirmed in Goritcheva, *Nous, convertis*. I draw your attention to the author's transcendent experience, chapter 2, especially 24–27.

11. Zielinski, "Une nouvelle génération," 79. A little further on (81), he alludes to a transcendent experience.

12. For the Bible, see Otto, *Idea of the Holy*, especially chapters 10 and 11, and Jacob, *Theology of the Old Testament*, "Manifestations of God," 73–85. For the history of religion and mysticism, a pioneer in the subject was Rudolf Otto: see Otto, *Mysticism East and West*.

Introduction

journey.[13] Modern because it is only since the eighteenth century that the value of personal religious experience, outside of liturgical or ecclesial settings, has been strongly emphasized.

Admittedly, many cultures—for example, those that have shaped Hinduism, Judaism, Christianity, and Islam—have had an interest in interiority. In the Latin Middle Ages, for example, the terms *experiri* and *experientia* were used to refer to experiencing the realities of the faith.[14] But it is only with the appearance of the religious genius of Luther, in a world where the individual was becoming more and more important, that we can see the emphasis move toward personal religious experience. At that point a new stage begins, where intolerance toward Jews, religious wars between Catholics and Protestants, as well as conflicts among Protestants bring about a weakening of ecclesial dogma and a strong emphasis on feelings. Thus, the eighteenth century witnesses a rise of Pietism in Germany, England, and the United States.

Two great theorists on the development and understanding of Pietism were very influential: Jonathan Edwards, an American, and Friedrich Schleiermacher, a German. Making use of and modifying Kantian philosophy, Schleiermacher was the first to describe and characterize what he called *the feeling of absolute dependence*. Furthermore, he is credited with understanding that this feeling can be distinguished from—but not separated from—all doctrinal considerations. This is an important discovery, even though we must challenge the idea that experience can exist in some pure state, outside of language. Lastly, he rightly places this experience in the realm of everyday life, not only in the realm of prayer.[15]

Although Edwards, Schleiermacher, and many researchers in the area of religious experience were churchmen, this field of research became more and more secularized as secular universities became involved. On the one hand, we now have access to countless studies that reflect many different approaches: historical,

---

13. Of course, people who are mature in their faith also have such experiences.

14. See Miquel, *Vocabulaire latin*.

15. Schleiermacher, *Christian Faith*, and *On Religion*.

Introduction

ethnological, phenomenological, philosophical, theological, psychological, and sociological. On the other hand, it is clear that the subject has caught the interest of the general public, as shown by the undeniable success of gurus, psychologists, and spiritual masters who write about this topic.[16]

The need to pay attention to this unique dimension of human experience is dictated by the fact that it provides a means of access to Mystery. Many are those who walk this path without any reference to official religions or to churches. These journeys are often legitimate, but they can also reveal some shortcomings. They must therefore be examined with both a sympathetic ear and a critical mind so as to "enter that path in which the divine depths and the human heights meet," as a world-renowned specialist on world religions put it.[17] This is done through identifying and analyzing from a phenomenological perspective, and then justifying on psychological and theological grounds, this place from which emerges, freshly and not surprisingly among those concerned, an unconditional respect for and sometimes even a great passion for the transcendent dimension.

This respect and this passion are found as much in individuals who believe in an impersonal divinity as in those who profess belief in a personal God. This explains why my approach in this book will be to use a very broad definition of the transcendent experience. The non-denominational nature of the definition will allow us to identify, in an ecumenical way, a meeting place for religions. More specifically, this is a starting point for the religious journey, and it contains great potential for inspiration and motivation. As Maslow so aptly pointed out, the peak-experience exerts a significant influence on the religious quest and on life in general.[18]

---

16. To mention but one example, the works of psychiatrist Karlfried Graf von Dürckheim, which are very popular in Germany and have been translated into English, French, and Spanish. See Roy, *Coherent Christianity*, chapter 12.

17. Panikkar, *Trinity*, xiv.

18. Maslow, *Psychology of Being*. For positive consequences, see chapters 6 and 7; for negative consequences, see chapter 8.

Introduction

What needs to be examined, therefore, is the emotional side of human openness to the infinite. Undoubtedly, the rational side of this openness is equally vital; it is based on a search for meaning in life. Even though the inquiry into this rational side will be treated more briefly in these pages, the reader must keep in mind that it is always connected to the emotional side. Indeed, the link between the rational and the emotional prevents the latter from locking itself into pure irrationality, which could not be integrated into the rest of the experience.

My inquiry is divided into four stages. The first three chapters will provide annotated accounts and will analyze elements and types of transcendent experience. Chapters 4 to 6 will present various positions taken by thinkers who have either rejected or provided positive critical assessments of what has often been called "oceanic feeling." Chapter 7 will tackle the problem of the validation of transcendent experiences. And finally, chapter 8 will ask questions about construing these experiences in terms of either an impersonal or a personal presence; it will also discuss the contribution of an interpretation that stems from faith in Jesus Christ.

1

The Feeling of What Transcends Us

Studies on, statistics about, and scientific research into the feeling of transcendence abound. But what exactly is this feeling? Let us start with some concrete life situations and listen to several witnesses to this reality. Here are three stories. I will comment on them only after we have heard them, one after another, without interruption.[1]

Three Accounts

The first was probably experienced in various degrees by many Quebecers during the opening ceremonies of the Olympic Games in July 1976 in Montreal. The event has taken on a special meaning for this witness.

> The spring of that year was a time of great tensions and confrontations in Quebec, especially in the health care and education sectors. The hopes sparked during the Quiet Revolution of the 1960s had been dashed, and many people in Quebec were keenly aware that economic

---

1. The three stories relate events that took place in Quebec. I believe they have a universal significance, to some extent like the novels of the English-speaking Jewish writer Mordecai Richler, whose stories are set in Montreal.

The Feeling of Transcendence, an Experience of God?

interests were reinforcing the barriers between different social classes. Many also bemoaned the extravagant expenses resulting from the construction of the stadium and other Olympic facilities.

Amid this climate of social division stood a vision of the Games as the celebration of a great universal fellowship. Some felt that they would express a boundless admiration for the energy, agility, and beauty of the human body. The coming together of athletes and representatives of so many countries was seen as a powerful symbol of unity, harmony, and peace. Many people looked forward to joining the festivities, but the more discerning ones were asking if the value of fellowship to be celebrated was real.

The high point of the opening ceremonies for the tens of thousands of spectators gathered at Olympic Stadium, and undoubtedly for the hundreds of millions watching on television, was the arrival of the Olympic flame—this sacred fire that had traveled to this place from across the globe. Physically, it had been lit at Olympia, in modern-day Greece; historically, it came from the Greece of antiquity, from ages long past. A relay of over a thousand runners, supported and accompanied by growing crowds, had carried the lit torch to Montreal. By this human journey, the Olympic ideal crossed space and time.

As the last of these runners enters the stadium, holding high the flame, the crowd rises as one and, carried away with excitement, utters a great unstoppable, resounding cry.

Twenty years later, I still tremble and am moved to tears as I relive that unforgettable moment. It unfolds before me as if it were only yesterday, and once again I can feel reverberating in me that surge of hope, that shared joy. The young runner is there; he moves forward surrounded by the crowd, holding high the symbol that captivates us and unites us to all the world's nations. For a few moments, our communion attains perfection. This extraordinary experience remains a high point for me.

The Feeling of What Transcends Us

Now let us turn to the story of a Quebec woman's spiritual discovery in a completely different context: within herself.[2]

> I was the eldest of the family. I had to take care of my younger siblings at home. My mother was sick. Later, after I was married, I stayed home to raise my own children. I am self-taught. I had a great passion for reading—books, newspapers, magazines. I was interested in everything I could get my hands on. It was my way of opening up to the world, traveling, escaping my little world. I loved to talk about things with my husband, with our friends, with my children. I often went to the public library.
>
> Then, at about the age of 37 or 38, I started looking more inwardly, as if I needed to empty myself, to reclaim myself with my own experience. I found the world to be more and more absurd. I was disheartened by human stupidity. I entered a great darkness. My work didn't really suffer. I never let anything show. My husband is a fragile man. My grown children were doing well enough, but were doing some seeking . . . they needed someone strong to give them some psychological security.
>
> In the depths of my being, I was pulling away from everything—the past, the present, the future. I had no religious life. Yet, God knows I had received one, lived it, swallowed it, but I remained curious about it, as I was curious about many things. Once in a while I would go to church, but inside I was miles away from it. When a person has read up on different religions, she becomes less gullible. My inner crisis was not a religious one. Rather, I had questions without any answers. Where is the world going? Where am I going?
>
> To tell you, to write about what happened, is very hard for me. I can't find the words. I am not a big believer in miracles, revelations, or things like that. Everything I had been taught eluded me. I had no points of reference to help me understand what was happening to me. I felt God within me, coming to me, without my having called him. As if telling me: "Yes, I was always with you, even

---

2. Grand'Maison and Lefebvre, *Génération bouc émissaire*, 53–54. Regarding the Quebec socio-cultural context in which such experiences take place, see chapter 13. Also see Grand'Maison et al., *Défi des générations*, chapter 2.

The Feeling of Transcendence, an Experience of God?

though you did not know it." My life suddenly started to make sense again, all my life in every detail, even my unanswered questions. It is not that I had an answer. It was something else that I can't easily describe. A joy, a fullness. Someone who had burst into my life like an unexpected and wonderful gift. Believing in God now seemed reasonable, even if I could not give reasons for it.

I talked about it with my husband and my friends. I really didn't have anything inspiring to say. Except that my life had changed even though I kept doing the things I did before. I was free. I was more mindful of others, more confident. There was a kind of certainty within me. A happiness that I can't describe.

I discovered another surprising thing. It turns out that my husband, and many of my friends, had also had an experience of God, each in their own way. They hadn't spoken of it to anyone. They were all very critical of the church, as I was.

I don't know if telling my story will be useful to you. For me, and for many other people, your pastoral activities just don't work! But did you know that there is an invisible faith, hidden within many people . . . that God passes through people's consciousness . . . that he is the Great Secretive One whom you can encounter more freely? What is the use of all your things, your rituals, your doctrines if you cannot recognize God within us? Maybe now we will get better at finding him in you. God has reclaimed his freedom. He is not trapped in the Bible, in the church, in religions. He is within men and women, above all in their lives. He follows us in silence. Every so often he makes his presence felt at the right moment. Are you ready to follow this God freely today, to go where he goes? It may be there that we shall meet.

Now let us listen to this final story, related to a difficult marital relationship. These events were experienced a number of years ago by a woman who was around thirty years old. She gave me permission to share her story, which she entitled "In order not to forget."

The Feeling of What Transcends Us

I am writing in order not to forget that one day I discovered in an unlikely way that I seemed to have entered into a consciousness that was completely distinct from the world in which I lived. What I was able to learn at that time, I swore that I would never forget.

At that time, I was involved in pastoral work in a parish and in a primary school. I was also taking part-time courses to complete my pastoral training. We were starting our fifth year of married life, and our marriage had been strained for several months. We had started couple's therapy in the fall, when suddenly in December I found out I was pregnant. My husband was not surprised that I would not consider terminating the pregnancy, as my first daughter had also been born under difficult circumstances (I was a single mother). He was unhappy about the pregnancy and clearly let me know that he did not want this child who, in his mind, was coming at a bad time. He respected my decision to go through with the pregnancy, but was not ready to enter into a relationship with this "intruder." In fact, he was not even sure he wished to continue his relationship with me.

The early months of my pregnancy were terrible. I felt abandoned and very insecure. Thankfully, I met with my therapist once a week and was surrounded by good friends. My husband was aloof, as he was totally preoccupied with trying to figure himself out and free himself from the vise that he felt was gradually tightening around him. I was also spending a lot of time trying to understand what he was going through and what we were going through. In my totally destabilized world, I was desperately seeking a fixed point. It seemed that my faith was no longer any help. I couldn't even draw upon my husband's faith, as he had told me that he no longer believed in God: "What's the point in believing in God?" he said to me. "When I need him, he isn't there. And how is your faith helping you?" His question left me speechless. It seemed that nothing I could say would make any difference. That question is like an open wound.

I spent hours crying over our crumbling relationship. Any hope I had was focused on my husband, from whom I desperately sought some sign of commitment.

The Feeling of Transcendence, an Experience of God?

Occasionally, my therapist tried to break through this illusion, to bring me back to myself. But I preferred to suffer. It was easier. I was not aware of trying to benefit from playing the victim. My friends and family were very sympathetic. I justified myself by thinking that the solution was in my husband's hands. I never thought that amid this tortuous journey, a great deliverance awaited us.

I was now halfway through my pregnancy. As part of my pastoral training, I decided to take a course on Providence. This session, which was held over two half-weekends, seems to have been an important catalyst for me. I remember that the session presented different ways of perceiving how God intervenes in the world. We demystified a certain view of God as intervening in and manipulating our freedom. The session also touched on the subject of human intentionality being open to the infinite and in search of global meaning, taking into account all the partial and contradictory meanings of life. Buoyed by these thoughts, I went home with some reading to do between the two weekends. That is when something really extraordinary happened to me.

That morning, as I often did, I was singing some religious hymns while I was cleaning the house. I put on some songs by the well-known French Christian singer Noël Colombier when I suddenly burst into tears as I sang along: "My whole life sings for you, Lord; may my whole life be prayer." As I looked out the window into the vast sky, I felt completely enfolded in the mystery of God. I felt consoled, reassured by a benevolent Presence who had come to place his deep peace within me, as if my whole existential reality had changed. I felt infinitely loved. Words from St. Paul came to me, as if gushing up from a spring: "Who will separate us from the love of Christ?" (Rom 8:35). A firm conviction arose from deep within me that gave me an all-embracing sense of security and put all my partial securities into perspective. My life suddenly found its meaning and security in God. I knew from within that I was no longer in danger. My hands unclenched and were ready to let go of all my illusory securities that were holding me hostage. Even if my husband were to leave me, I knew I would get through it. I felt that I was being carried by caring hands and no longer feared anything. I did not know why or how all this happened to me, but I accepted it as a great gift for which I was infinitely grateful.

The experience was so intense and euphoric, I didn't really know how and to whom I should talk about it. I was very aware that not everyone would be able to understand what had happened to me. I remember that I first shared my experience with a priest friend who had a keen interest in conversion and adult faith. I needed someone who could help me understand what was happening to me. I shared with him my biases and my skepticism about dramatic conversions, while at the same time being convinced of the very real and beneficial nature of what I was going through. I was trying to figure out why I had had such an experience and what it might have to do with my overall faith journey. He listened to me very carefully and helped me place this event in a larger context. He explained that such occurrences are fairly common, though they are often not discussed openly. Some people experience them more intensely than others, depending on their personality and their nature. However, such intense moments do not determine the quality of a person's spiritual life. They can be short-lived and bear little fruit. It all depends on how they are interpreted and reinvested in a person's day-to-day life. Indeed, I felt that this euphoric state would subside and give way one day to a naked faith.

During the second weekend of the training session, I also shared my experience with my teacher. I thanked him, since I had a sense that the course I was taking was somehow part of what had happened. I truly welcomed what was happening as a free gift that had nothing to do with any effort or merit on my part; in fact, I was sure that God had not overridden my freedom. The best analogy I could find for what was going on was that of two intersecting wavelengths. As I searched, I had met God, who was searching for me. If I had not tuned my radio transmitter to this frequency, he could not have reached me to communicate what he wanted me to know about

The Feeling of Transcendence, an Experience of God?

Him. Global Security had contacted me, unleashing in me a peace and a strength that I could not understand.

This invaluable encounter gave me the courage to move forward into the unknown, even though the future remained uncertain. I then decided to speak with my husband to try to explain to him that I no longer needed him and that he was free to leave. My relationship with him was no longer based on need, but how could I explain to him that I loved him in a different way? He was very unsettled by my words. If I no longer needed him, what was left? However, he quickly felt the freeing effects of my new stance toward him: in this way, freely and gradually, he started working at our relationship. He grew closer to me and to the child I was carrying and eventually was charmed by this little being who came into the world; he greeted the baby with open arms. By learning to love my husband for who he was and not only for what he did for me, our love was transformed and grew more free.

At times, anxiety and insecurities once again caused stormy weather to hit my life, but in the deep waters the sea stays calm and peaceful. This belief is rooted in the deepest part of my being: "Who will separate us from the love of Christ? Will hardship, or distress, or persecution, or famine, or nakedness, or peril, or sword? ... For I am convinced that neither death, nor life, nor angels, nor rulers, nor things present, nor things to come, nor powers, nor height, nor depth, nor anything else in all creation, will be able to separate us from the love of God in Christ Jesus our Lord" (Rom 8:35, 38–39).

Through this wonderful experience and what followed, I have discovered in an existential way the meaning of resurrection. I had passed through death to be resurrected. I now understood that faith in God isn't about avoiding death; rather, it allows a person to move through death in order to come out stronger and freer than before. Since then, the Paschal Mystery has been at the core of my faith, and the Scriptures are the interpretative lens through which I understand my entire life. My journey is a long Exodus leading to freedom, and I know

now that God opens the way and provides manna in the desert.

I imagine that some readers were able to relate to one of these three stories, in some way, through one of the events described here. In reading these stories, other readers, although they may not have seen themselves exactly, will have thought of comparable events in their own lives. Still others will remember that someone they know once shared with them a similar experience. Some readers will admit to being fascinated, even stunned, by these disconcerting inner journeys. They raise the question of whether to enthusiastically embrace such journeys or skeptically keep them at bay. These experiences are perplexing; we don't know what to think. We may ask questions such as these: What is the point of these experiences? Are they always obvious? Do they sweep away all our doubts? What conclusions can we come to when we explore, by trial and error, what has happened?

A common feature emerges from these three accounts. We are in the presence of a feeling that is stronger than usual, and whose tone varies. It is the crowd's exuberant communion as it drinks from the cup of universal fellowship, as expressed through athletic beauty and a torch lit from a time-honored fire; or the joy, the unfathomable happiness of feeling God in oneself—a certainty that sets us free; or the exhilaration at being totally enveloped, consoled, and reassured by a caring Presence who brings us deep peace.

Another thing to note: this feeling leads to a discovery, to an *insight* that comes as an answer to a concern that we noticed sometime before the experience. It is a comprehensive solution—felt intuitively—to a problem with which a person is struggling: whether it be the social issues in Quebec at the time of the Olympic Games; the sense of the absurd in the face of human stupidity that raises questions like "Where is the world going? Where am I going?"; or the fear that your husband will leave you because you are pregnant.

In addition to this, the second and third stories contain a few striking impressions. First, the fact that human words are barely adequate in conveying such an unusual experience. Second,

The Feeling of Transcendence, an Experience of God?

appreciation or gratitude in response to the unexpected and wonderful gift that has been given. Finally, there are after-effects: greater personal autonomy, an openness to others, a kind of trust. The author of the third account writes: "Global Security had contacted me, unleashing in me a peace and a strength that I could not understand."

Affinities and Differences

In line with previous researchers who have studied religious phenomena, it is important to specify which kind of experiences will be the focus of this study. In doing this, we will both limit the scope of the investigation and discover some overlap with other similar phenomena.

Following the approach of a number of experts, I will not consider certain phenomena to be transcendent experiences: "visions, auditions, locutions, telepathy, telekinesis, or any other praeternatural phenomenon."[3] This list is from R. C. Zaehner, who distinguishes between these phenomena and what he calls proper mystical experiences. This distinction is confirmed by Greeley, who divides the *paranormal* into two categories: (1) the *parapsychical*, which includes déjà vu, extrasensory perception, clairvoyance, and contact with the dead, and (2) the *mystical*, which covers the field of what I call transcendent experiences.[4] Likewise, Robert Crookall differentiates between those who have experiences of at-onement: "psychics," who have the ability to heal, and "mystics," who reach a certain spiritual level.[5] While non-mystical phenomena can be impressive, they do not in themselves put people in contact with something that is utterly beyond them. These phenomena open up to the infinite only if they are linked to a transcendent experience.

---

3. Zaehner, *Mysticism Sacred and Profane*, 32. This opinion is also held by Stace, *Mysticism and Philosophy*, 47–55, and Johnston, *Silent Music*, 72–73, who quotes subject matter experts like Guibert and Suzuki.

4. See Greeley, *Sociology of the Paranormal*, table of contents and 43.

5. Crookall, *Interpretation of Cosmic*, 128–30.

The Feeling of What Transcends Us

The transcendent experience is equivalent to what many authors, especially English-speaking ones, call a *mystical experience*. However, to ensure clarity, I will avoid this latter expression, as it conveys a sense of something exceptional: a striking revelation, or the notion of an enduring divine presence, which is associated with individuals who have an advanced prayer life. The word *ecstasy* will also be avoided. The experiences studied in this book are not necessarily ecstasies, which involve losing a sense of one's surroundings, although ecstasy is almost always a transcendent experience.[6]

The same thing must be said about the idea of *life after death*, discussed by philosopher and psychiatrist Raymond Moody. Of the stories he presents, some provide no indication of encounters with something that is beyond us in every respect. Other stories, meanwhile, use unambiguous expressions indicating that we are dealing with transcendent experiences. A reader can only be struck by the unique and unparalleled nature of the perceived light, as well as by feelings of completeness associated with it.[7]

I will use the term *transcendent experience* rather than *religious experience*. William James wrongly considers as typical of a religious experience, or as the best of religion, the powerful emotions that some people feel when they are alone.[8] A proper phenomenological approach that takes into account all religious data cannot glorify strong emotion as if it were greater than belief in a personal God, than the thoughts and pious sentiments not directly related to a sense of the infinite, or even than belonging to an

---

6. See Laski, *Ecstasy*. The meaning given by the author to the word *ecstasy* is weaker and more general than that generally given by others, in English as well as in French. This meaning is nearly equivalent to my concept of transcendent experience.

7. Moody, *Life after Life*, 48–49, 56; see also Moody, *Reflections*. Heaney, *Sacred and the Psychic*, presents numerous inquiries that confirm the prevalence of this experience (see chapter 8); he considers it "a mystical experience in the broad sense" (147). Along the same lines, see Vernette, *Réincarnation*, 100–113.

8. James, *Varieties of Religious Experience*.

The Feeling of Transcendence, an Experience of God?

institution—a group or a church.[9] Moreover, the transcendent experience does not always correspond to the phenomena described by James. Its specific character lies in opening the human being to something other than what everyday life offers, in having a striking awareness of the non-finite, though not necessarily through a feeling that completely overwhelms one's sensibilities.

I will also abstain from using the expression *transcendental experience*,[10] to avoid any confusion with the transcendental aspect of knowledge and of love, as found in Kant, Rahner, and Lonergan. I will as well set aside the term *experience of the transcendent*, which suggests that the transcendent is an entity, a being among beings, with whom a person could have a direct encounter. *Experience of our transcendence* has merit, but this wording accounts for only one aspect of a two-sided phenomenon. The two sides are our mind that is open to the infinite, and the reality to which our mind is open. *Transcendent experience* (or *feeling of transcendence*), on the other hand, immediately conveys this important and rich ambiguity, this convergence of the subjective aspect and the objective aspect, which will be discussed later.

Other expressions touch on what is meant in this study by *transcendent experience*. The Canadian psychiatrist R. M. Bucke (1837–1902) spoke of a *cosmic consciousness*, which equals "a consciousness of the cosmos, that is, of the life and order of the universe," along which "occurs an intellectual enlightenment or illumination" as well as "a state of moral exaltation, an indescribable feeling of elevation, elation and joyousness," and "a sense of immortality, a consciousness of eternal life."[11] I will use the adjective *aesthetic* in the next chapter to describe our first type of transcendent experience.

---

9. See a critique of James by Jean Mouroux, as summarized in Bourdeau, "Jean Mouroux," 4–6 and 12.

10. As is found in Margolis and Elifson, "Typology," 61–67. What I call the experience of transcendence corresponds to their Factor I.

11. Bucke, *Cosmic Consciousness*, 3. The work was first published in 1901. On pages 9–10, the author tells the story of his experience of cosmic consciousness that occurred in 1873.

The Feeling of What Transcends Us

Another classic book on the subject—perhaps the best known—is Rudolf Otto's *The Idea of the Holy*, which enthusiastically describes the life-changing encounter with *the holy* (in German: *das Heilige*), triggering the feeling of the *numinous* (from the Latin *numen*: divine majesty). Otto explains that this encounter is both positive and negative. Indeed, the mystery has two aspects: it is *tremendum*—that is, awful or "terrifying," the object of fear, even dread; and it is *fascinosum*—that is, attractive and fascinating. In writing about a transcendent experience, author Julien Green evokes both aspects when he writes, "It was a peculiar sensation, halfway between pleasure and fright."[12]

Psychiatrist Karlfried Graf von Dürckheim speaks of the *experience of Being*, which consists in attaining Life, Meaning, and Love beyond death, beyond the interplay of meaning and non-meaning, and beyond the alternation of sympathy and antipathy that affects the existential self.[13] This division more or less equals the three types of anxiety described by Paul Tillich: the anxiety of fate and death, of emptiness and loss of meaning, and of guilt and condemnation. Faced with this triple anxiety, the courage to be, supported by the power of being, enables a person to base their self-affirmation on trust in Being.[14]

The sociologist Peter Berger, meanwhile, is interested in "signals of transcendence"; he finds them in certain "prototypical human gestures," by which he means "certain reiterated acts and experiences that appear to express essential aspects of man's being, of the human animal as such."[15] In chapter 3, we will consider the examples that Berger gives.

Psychologist Abraham Maslow classifies the "mystic, or oceanic, or nature experience" among what he calls "peak-experiences," which are not responses to needs, but rather allow a person to strive for fullness of being.[16]

12. Green, *Then Shall the Dust*, 258; see 257–58.
13. von Dürckheim, *Two-fold Origin*, 51–53.
14. Tillich, *Courage to Be*, chapters 2 and 6.
15. Berger, *Rumor of Angels*, 65–66; see 65–90.
16. Maslow, *Psychology of Being*, 84.

The Feeling of Transcendence, an Experience of God?

In this chapter, we began to acknowledge various transcendent experiences and perhaps even to see ourselves in them. We also realized that a number of authors have written on this subject, each using a distinctive vocabulary and insisting on particular aspects. The three stories presented in this chapter incorporate many elements or stages that are well worth exploring. That will be the work of the next chapter.

2

Slow-Motion Replay

To gain a fuller appreciation of the richness of the stories already presented, and of those to be explored in upcoming chapters, we will look at a slow-motion replay of the transcendent experience and describe its stages in detail. In the three stories presented in chapter 1, the core of the experience—feeling and discovery—followed a certain preoccupation and circumstance that were both the preparation for and the occasion of the experience. This core was followed by an interpretation through which the person's view of himself or herself shifted with respect to the rest of the person's life, and by a fruit, such as a newly gained sense of peace or security.

After an extended effort to remain faithful to the numerous works I have consulted, and following years of discussions with various groups, I have come to discern six elements that constitute a transcendent experience: preparation, occasion, feeling, discovery, interpretation, and fruit. The analysis on which I embark here draws on phenomenology: the intent is to simply reflect the phenomena without, in these next three chapters, making any statement about their validity. Thus, the elements of lived experiences will be presented in a manner that, while avoiding the epistemological aspiration and complexity of Husserl's approach, holds fast

The Feeling of Transcendence, an Experience of God?

to its desire to examine the experience in the spirit of *epoché*—that is, the intentional hiatus, the bracketing, the suspension of any value judgment on the realities in question. The philosophical and theological neutrality that will mark the first part of this inquiry does not, however, exclude a clear affinity for the experience itself, regardless of what one might think, at this initial stage, of the real or illusory object to which it might be directed.[1]

Constitutive Elements

First, *preparation* is the cognitive and affective context that conditions—without inflexibly determining—the forthcoming experience. It is constituted by the lifestyle, personality, views, concerns, problems, and questions of an individual or group. Although the experience will add new content, these predispositions influence what is going to happen. They constitute a prior readiness that makes possible the decisive feeling. This readiness consists in a sense of dissatisfaction and at times an active search. Thus, there exists a tension, an unrest filled with promise, an openness—admitted or denied, peaceful or conflictual—within the person, who, generally without realizing it, is preparing for a breakthrough.

In the context, somewhat different from our own, of the "existential encounter" with a revelatory text, Rudolf Bultmann stresses the need for a preunderstanding (*Vorverständnis*), which he describes as a "very vague knowledge," a "peculiarly not-knowing knowledge."[2] He expresses quite well the paradoxical relation between anticipation and discovery:

> But, to be sure, I can know what light and life are even when it is dark and I do not see anything. Even the blind man knows what light is. And I can know what love and friendship are even if I have not found love and have not met any friend. Thus I know what revelation is without having found revelation – and yet I do not *really* know it. For the blind man also only really knows what light

---

1. See de Muralt, *Idea of Phenomenology*, see "The Cogita[t]um," 259–80.
2. Bultmann, *Existence and Faith*, 70, 75, 347.

Slow-Motion Replay

is when he sees it, and the person who is friendless and unloved only really knows what friendship and love are when he finds a friend and is given love.[3]

The preparation is both long term and short term. In the long term, it can involve days, weeks, or years during which something begins to ferment within those involved. In the short term, the preparation relates to the physical and psychological situation in which they find themselves just before the experience. This twofold preparation is as necessary for the transcendent experience as it is for an artistic endeavor, as phenomenologist Mikel Dufrenne explains:

> An immediacy of fact does, of course, exist. There are a beginning to perception and a first contact with the object of such a sort that the object often seems to offer itself from that first moment. But this is not an absolute beginning. We go to the object with an entire array of past experiences which form our particular culture. The musical work is certainly new to the conductor who promptly grasps its structure and meaning in a single reading of the score, but his look is hardly new.[4]

The second element is *occasion*, which is, in a given situation, what sets the experience in motion. It can be an event, an object on which a person focuses, an image, a vision, a dream, a thought, a phrase heard or recalled, a vista, a painting or piece of music, vigorous athletic exercise, an intense pleasure, a physical or psychological shock such as an accident or bad news, or the opposite, good news, a source of great joy. The occasion belongs to our everyday world. Peter Berger writes of this when he presents his signals of transcendence: "By signals of transcendence I mean phenomena that are to be found within the domain of our 'natural' reality but that appear to point beyond that reality."[5]

---

3. Bultmann, *Existence and Faith*, 71.
4. Dufrenne, *Phenomenology*, 417–18.
5. Berger, *Rumor of Angels*, 65–66.

The Feeling of Transcendence, an Experience of God?

Jean-Pierre Valla provides a very good explanation of the occasions, factors, or stimuli that trigger what he calls the *oceanic feeling*, which to me is equivalent to a form of transcendent experience, which I call aesthetic, that I will describe in chapter 3. The common denominator turns out to be the loss of normal reference points, whether spatial, temporal, or other.[6] For example, the sudden widening of our visual field (at the top of a mountain or facing the ocean), the connection to the endlessness of the ages (in a historical setting or during a traditional religious service), the presence of a superior power (physical, psychological, or parapsychological), the breadth and complexity of a musical composition (an organ piece heard in a church), a distancing from one's regular environment (during a trip or a sexual encounter), or the total focusing on a single point (either accidentally or deliberately, such as during meditation).

The third element, *feeling*, which is at the core of the experience, plays a role that is similar to the one in the following passage from *Siddhartha*, by Hermann Hesse:

> As Siddhartha left the grove in which the Buddha, the Perfect One, remained, in which Govinda remained, he felt that he had also left his former life behind him in the grove. As he slowly went on his way, his head was full of this thought. He reflected deeply, until this feeling completely overwhelmed him and he reached a point where he recognized causes; for to recognize causes, it seemed to him, is to think, and through thought alone feelings become knowledge, and are not lost, but become real and begin to mature.[7]

From that feeling, Siddhartha gains a deeper understanding of himself; in particular, he is freed from the need for a spiritual master.

Two passages from Mikel Dufrenne's book, cited above, will further highlight the role played by feeling.[8] Although Dufrenne

6. Valla, *Les états étranges*, 41–90.
7. Hesse, *Siddhartha*, "Awakening," 30.
8. Dufrenne, *Phenomenology*, 375–79 and 398–407.

does not have the transcendent experience in mind, I believe that the aesthetic feeling he explores comes closest to the feeling of transcendence in human existence. The close similarity between the two will therefore be our starting point. The feeling he presents belongs to the aesthetic experience and differs from three other orientations that human intentionality can adopt: mere presence to the perceived object, theoretical representation, and emotion that leads to action.

Aesthetic feeling goes much further than mere presence to the perceived object, because it enters into the intimacy and depth of the object. Going beyond a simple glance, this penetration calls forth from the subject an interiority, a commitment, a participation, a communion. Moving beyond the superficial impressions of mere presence, the person who has an artistic experience lets himself or herself be touched in their entire being. A mutual gift is exchanged between subject and object: the object does not really belong to me unless I belong to it. For this to happen, I must yield to it with generosity, trust, fervor, and even love.

Nor is the aesthetic feeling a matter of what Dufrenne calls representation. The latter sorts, analyzes, and leads to abstract reflection. Of course, such reflection can assist with artistic appreciation. But the study of art alternates with the aesthetic experience, rather than being a stage in the experience itself. When it comes to feeling, the world is felt; with representation, it is thought.

Finally, Dufrenne distinguishes between emotion—which leads to action—and artistic feeling. This distinction is grounded in the difference between practical living and art. In practical living, emotion results in action; in art, feeling leads to contemplation. Thus, Dufrenne points out that fear is not to be confused with the feeling of what is horrific; merriment is not the feeling of what is comic; terror or pity is not the feeling of what is tragic. He adds that great artists spark in spectators not the emotion, but the feeling—that is, a particular mode of being, some kind of sense. For example, Racine possesses and communicates the sense of tragedy; Daumier, the sense of the grotesque; and Wagner, the sense of wonder.

The Feeling of Transcendence, an Experience of God?

These three characteristics that Dufrenne notes in aesthetic feeling are also found in the feeling of transcendence. The latter is more than mere presence to an object and consists in neither a representation nor an action. It indicates a kind of depth and commitment not unlike that of the artistic experience. Located at the core of the transcendent experience, the feeling is deep and engaging enough to make possible a breakthrough, a stunning discovery.

Discovery is the fourth element of the transcendent experience and, once again, Dufrenne is a helpful guide.[9] Because his phenomenology does not rule out objectivity, he avoids making the mistake of approaching feeling in a subjectivist way. What happens to the human subject is always correlative to an object. Dufrenne highlights the noetic function of feeling, which reveals a world. In one and the same movement, we can subjectively open up a world and objectively open ourselves to that world. Aesthetic feeling opens us up in this way, based on this twofold experience. Because of its intentionality, that is, its active reception of reality, this feeling allows us to transcend the self.

We will now explore the aspect of the feeling and discovery of transcendence that eludes the analogy I have just outlined. It is the strong impression of being in touch with something that absolutely transcends us. This rather general statement seems to me to be the most all-encompassing one we could use to express what so many narratives convey. Most often, the authors of these narratives do not reduce this mysterious unknown to a perceived object. They instead speak of an indefinable dimension or presence. Furthermore, they distinguish the occasion—which may be an object that is perceived—from what it triggered: the feeling of being open to something absolutely transcendent.

The feeling in question therefore has a special property: an openness to something that seems unlimited: life, love, goodness, evil, light, darkness, sea, nature, cosmos, space, time, etc. It thus differs from ordinary religious feelings, which do not include this sense of the infinite. Let us note that the difference between

---

9. Dufrenne, *Phenomenology*, 376–79 and 404–5.

Slow-Motion Replay

them is not a matter of intensity, since some powerful feelings do not refer to anything transcendent. Even though it is not always overwhelming, the feeling that opens one up to the infinite cannot pass unnoticed, although the person having the experience is often unable to name it. They will indeed be aware of the unique character of the feeling that has touched, moved, and taken hold of them. The impression of being carried beyond the limits of the day-to-day is at the heart of the experience. One feels that it would be futile to attempt to artificially constrain this discovery, that it commands unconditional respect.

This raises a question: Discovery of what? At this stage of our inquiry, it would be premature to want to determine the ontological status of this "something that absolutely transcends us." Phenomenology does, however, allow us to assert already that the human subject experiences its openness to the non-finite or the in-finite, understood as a negation of that which is finite, limited. Perceived through feeling, the consciousness of this openness separates the human being from other animals. Drawing on axiology, the philosophical study of the nature of value, we can add that the human being is sensitive to a concrete value, but to what is unlimited in that value.

As an example, let us turn to the words of a musician who speaks of the coming out of oneself that happens through music, both secular and sacred:

> Sacred music, like anything that is sacred, lies apart, beyond, within us but, as it were, carrying us outside of ourselves. It possesses a particular character that in some way transports us above the created, the physical, the sensory. It reaches the highest and most immaterial part of us. It takes us out of ourselves, it turns us toward the other; if you will: an *Other*, by its ability to silence within us the preoccupations, the concerns, the difficulties of everyday life. Of course, you will object, saying that any beautiful music can have the same beneficial effects. Without question. And here we may be dealing with a sacred aspect of all good music . . . . But it seems to me that music that is truly sacred pushes the human

The Feeling of Transcendence, an Experience of God?

being even further and more fully toward heights that skim the lost paradise to which even a soul that is barely religious aspires.[10]

The fifth element of the transcendent experience is *interpretation*, that is, reflection. There are two kinds. First is a thought process intimately associated with the experience, a kind of mirroring of the event. It is a reflection in the sense that it reflects the experience. Dufrenne speaks of this when he emphasizes the complementarity between feeling and the reflective act.[11] Thought then seeks to name the experience, while remaining very close to it, letting itself be guided and enlightened by the feeling, whose role is to reveal. This "sympathetic reflection" tries to recapture the lived event, to break down what is given as a unit in the event.

The second form of reflection is no longer just a reflection *of* the experience, but a reflection *on* the experience. It is rooted in the desire to understand what has happened, to grasp its freshness and significance, and to situate it with respect to the rest of human life. From intuitive, the reflection becomes interrogative, evaluative, even suspicious of what has taken place. This critical distance taken in confronting one's experience is rooted in a desire for honesty in the search for the truth, value, and ramifications of the experience.

Both kinds of reflection are conditioned by the worldview of a person before the experience. To express a lived experience, people inevitably use intellectual categories and words that are familiar. It is well known that both of these shape the thinking of individuals and groups. However, a lived experience need not be shackled by a fixed worldview. Through the impact of a profound experience, a person may use categories, images, and words in creative ways. Feeling and thought can then lead the person to express relatively new content.

The sixth and final element in transcendent experience is the *fruit*—the benefit a person gets from it in terms of knowledge,

---

10. Skinner, "Musique et paroles sacrées," 556–57.
11. Dufrenne, *Phenomenology*, 415–25.

wisdom, attitude, and motivation. It may be expressed in terms of transformation, conversion, a change in perspective, or a response to a summons perceived in the experience itself. As was the case for reflection, the fruit may emerge immediately from the experience or ripen over time. The first fruit can be seen as part of the experience, and the second as belonging to a later stage. This offers a distinction between the transcendent experience (including its immediate fruit) and the in-depth transformation (equivalent to a fruit cultivated with care and perseverance).

A Classic Text

These six elements are found in the Bhagavad Gita,[12] a classic text composed in India around the first or second century BC. Chapter 11 of this long, remarkably deep poem presents a transcendent experience which contains frequent attribution of infinite characteristics to God, as well as a complementarity between fascination and dread—a typical complementarity in the thought of Rudolf Otto, as we saw at the end of chapter 1.

The element of *preparation* is found in the sense of futility felt by the great archer Arjuna, son of Pandu, on the eve of a military battle. On the battlefield, he sees two armies of fellow citizens about to face each other in combat. On both sides are warriors that he knows and holds in high esteem. The element of *occasion* that triggers the experience is the need to set his duty as a warrior in relation to religious wisdom. That is why he makes an extremely bold request:

> (3) Even as You have described [your] Self to be, so must it be, O Lord Most High; [but] fain would I see the form of You as Lord, O [All-]Highest Person.
>
> (4) If, Lord, You think that I can see You thus, then show me, Lord of creative power (yoga), [this] Self [of yours] which does not pass away.

---

12. *The Bhagavad-Gita*. My reading was guided by Aurobindo, *Essays on the Gita*, and Zaehner's work.

The Feeling of Transcendence, an Experience of God?

The Blessed Lord said:

(7) Do you today the whole universe behold centred here in One, with all that it contains of moving and unmoving things; [behold it] in my body, and whatever else you fain would see.

(8) But never will you be able to see Me with this your [natural] eye. A celestial eye I'll give you, behold my power [yoga] as Lord!

Concerning the revelation that is about to begin, the narrator offers the following comment:

(12) If in [bright] heaven together should arise the shining brilliance of a thousand suns, then would that perhaps resemble the brilliance of that [God] so great of Self.

(13) Then did the son of Pandu see the whole [wide] universe in One converged, there in the body of the God of gods, yet divided out in multiplicity.

Arjuna said:

(15) O God, the gods in your body I behold and all the hosts of every kind of being; Brahma, the lord, [I see] throned on the lotus-seat, celestial serpents and all the [ancient] seers.

(16) Arms, bellies, mouths, and eyes all manifold – so do I see You wherever I may look, – infinite your form! End, middle, or again beginning I cannot see in You, O Monarch Universal, [manifest] in every form!

The following verses reveal that Arjuna's dominant feeling is horror at the imminent bloodshed, a horror that his transcendent experience allows him to transpose onto God. Arjuna said:

(23) Gazing upon your mighty form with its myriad mouths, eyes, arms, thighs, feet, bellies, and sharp, gruesome tusks, the worlds [all] shudder [in affright], – how much more I!

(27) [The main warriors of our camp] rush [blindly] into your [gaping] mouths that with their horrid tusks strike

Slow-Motion Replay

[them] with terror. Some stick in the gaps between your teeth, – see them! – their heads to powder ground!

(30) On every side You lick, lick up, – devouring, – worlds, universes, everything, – with burning mouths. Vishnu! your dreadful rays of light fill the whole universe with flames-of-glory, scorching [everywhere].

The main discovery is thus Arjuna's vision of Krishna (Vishnu, Vasudeva, the Blessed Lord) as the great destroyer. He sees God as incorporating all this destruction, as the necessity that justifies the massacre, as the support and order underpinning the universe, as recapitulating plurality in unity as well as all the stages of time. This interpretation—especially the idea that the universe is unfolded time and again beyond the divine and absorbed back into it—comes from Hindu and Buddhist themes that the author weaves into his work.

In the end, the horrific aspect of the experience is counterbalanced by a reassuring one.

The Blessed Lord said:
(49) You need not tremble nor need your spirit be perplexed though you have seen this form of mine, so awful, grim. Banish all fear, be glad at heart: behold again that [same familiar] form [you knew].

And the narrator adds:
(50) Thus speaking did the son of Vasudeva show his [human] form to Arjuna again, comforting him in his fear. For once again the great-souled [Krishna] assumed the body of a friend.

Having received the grace to contemplate the universe from the perspective of "the celestial eye," having discovered Krishna's terrifying power, and then having been reassured in his relationship with Krishna by once again seeing his benign form, Arjuna resolves to do his knightly duty and fight for the side on which destiny has placed him. The fruit of his transcendent experience is thus moral courage based on a mystical vision.

The Feeling of Transcendence, an Experience of God?

This chapter offered a slow-motion replay of the stages that make up a transcendent experience. Now that we can better appreciate its various elements, we turn our inquiry in the next chapter to the various types of such an experience.

3

Families of Mindsets

In the previous chapter, we discovered in a classic Eastern text the six elements of a transcendent experience. To appreciate the depth and variety of such an experience, we will now turn to contemporary Western narratives. I suggest going a step further and adding four types, or families, to the six elements. After years of trial and error and revision, I have come to the conclusion that transcendent experiences can be divided into four main types: aesthetic, ontological, ethical, and interpersonal.

Why complicate things in this way? It may assist us in pinpointing the factor that explains the variety of these experiences and discovering where it comes from. As we will see, this factor is found in the two elements that precede the crucial feeling: the preparation and the occasion.

The first type—*aesthetic*—has to do with nature or the cosmos. It is the oceanic feeling: people then feel that they are in deep harmony with the world or have a sense of being part of a greater whole. It can also be the discovery that one is at the mercy of destructive physical forces that seem all-powerful. The second type—*ontological*—relates to being and non-being. One sees oneself as intellectually secure and grounded in an order of reality that lies beyond contingency, or one perceives oneself as without

The Feeling of Transcendence, an Experience of God?

recourse before non-meaning and nothingness. The third type—*ethical*—pertains to values. A person grasps the inexhaustible appeal of a value such as justice, solidarity, fraternity, or devotion; or feels extremely vulnerable in the face of an anti-value such as injustice, betrayal, indifference, or hostility. The fourth type—*interpersonal*—is found in the specifically human sphere of life. Stemming from a desire for or a refusal of communion, a person finds a superhuman basis for this human-to-human relationship, or feels in touch with a unique presence, or else flees this presence when it is perceived as a threat.

The principle underlying this classification is that each type is linked to a fundamental area of human life: the relation to nature, to being, to values, or to people. Nature appears mainly (but not exclusively) to our senses; being, to our intellect; values, to our sensibility; and people, to our heart. When we examine accounts of transcendent experiences, we see, however, that some of them reveal characteristics of more than one type.

The key to this classification into types of experiences turns out to be the elements of preparation and occasion. These guide the transcendent experience. Thus, the first type depends on a concern with the body, health, physical effort and rest, the environment, birth, and death. The second type depends on a concern with the meaning of life, the passage of time, the ephemerality of all things, the future of the human race.[1] The third type depends on a concern with self-realization, life within the family, community, or society, the voice of conscience, moral failure, and evil. Lastly, the fourth type depends on a concern for communication, the desire to love and be loved, the hunger for happiness, the possibility of fulfillment.

---

1. In the first chapter of Barzel, *Mystique de l'Ineffable*, the author suggests an interesting typology. His first type of experiences, "contingency-immortality," corresponds to my second type; his second type, "cosmic resonance," corresponds to my first. His other two types shed very little light on the subject, as they are too closely tied to the interpretation given in the accounts themselves. Thus, the critical step of identifying the characteristics of each type, which is what I will attempt to do by looking at the situation and the occasion, which are identifiable through the interpretation.

Families of Mindsets

Examples

The first type—aesthetic—which is found in the realm of nature, corresponds to Emmanuel Kant's description of the sublime. Two works in particular of this great philosopher of the Enlightenment express his thoughts on the subject of the feeling of the infinite: *Observations on the Feeling of the Beautiful and Sublime*[2] and, later in his life, *Critique of the Power of Judgment*.[3] His reflections must be placed within a long literary and psychological tradition that goes all the way back to Longinus, who would influence Kant through the works of Edmund Burke.[4] Thus we find in Longinus the statement that nature "implanted in our minds from the start an irresistible desire for anything which is great and, in relation to ourselves, supernatural."[5] He adds: "The universe therefore is not wide enough for the range of human speculation and intellect. Our thoughts often travel beyond the boundaries of our surroundings."[6]

Kant suggests in *Observations* that the feeling of the sublime varies:

> The sublime is in turn of different sorts. The feeling of it is sometimes accompanied with some dread or even melancholy, in some cases merely with quiet admiration and in yet others with a beauty spread over a sublime prospect. I will call the first the **terrifying sublime**, the second the **noble**, and the third the **magnificent**.[7]

In his *Critique of the Power of Judgment*, Kant points out that the experience of the sublime has two parts: displeasure, followed by pleasure; repulsion, followed by attraction; a brief interruption of life force, followed by an outpouring of it.[8] Anticipating Rudolf Otto, he speaks of "what is repellent for the sensibility, but which

2. Originally published in 1764. Kant, *Observations*.
3. Originally published in 1790. Kant, *Critique*.
4. Originally published in 1757. Burke, *Philosophical Enquiry*.
5. Longinus, *On Sublimity*, 42.
6. Longinus, *On Sublimity*, 42.
7. Kant, *Observations*, 16. (Emphasis in bold in the original.)
8. Kant, *Critique*, §23, §27.

The Feeling of Transcendence, an Experience of God?

is at the same time attractive for it."[9] Kant gives as examples the shapeless mountain masses,[10] the horrible visage of the wide ocean enraged by storms, and nature's chaos and its wildest and most unruly order and devastation,[11] such as hurricanes, volcanoes, and waterfalls.[12]

Let us now leave behind the eighteenth century and move to the experiences alluded to by Jean-Paul Sartre and Martin Heidegger. They belong to the second type—ontological. In his novel *Nausea*, Sartre presents the vision of existence[13] that Antoine Roquetin had while fascinated by the roots of a chestnut tree, a "black, knotty mass, entirely beastly, which frightened me."[14] Existence seems like something "*In the way*,"[15] "the key to my Nauseas . . . the absolute or the absurd,"[16] a "filth."[17] The author of the story, "motionless and icy, plunged in a horrible ecstasy,"[18] describes his reaction in this way:

> And I—soft, weak, obscene, digesting, juggling with dismal thoughts—I, too, was *In the way*. Fortunately, I didn't feel it, although I realized it, but I was uncomfortable because I was afraid of feeling it (even now I am afraid—afraid that it might catch me behind my head and lift me up like a wave). I dreamed vaguely of killing myself to wipe out at least one of these superfluous lives. But even my death would have been *In the way*.[19]

---

9. Kant, *Critique*, §28.
10. Kant, *Critique*, §26.
11. Kant, *Critique*, §23.
12. Kant, *Critique*, §28.
13. Sartre, *Nausea*, 127–35.
14. Sartre, *Nausea*, 127.
15. Sartre, *Nausea*, 128.
16. Sartre, *Nausea*, 129.
17. Sartre, *Nausea*, 134.
18. Sartre, *Nausea*, 131.
19. Sartre, *Nausea*, 128.

Families of Mindsets

Given the *purely* negative quality of all this, a person might consider this vision,[20] this fascination,[21] that is to say the intuition of contingency, as an incomplete transcendent experience, an aborted experience.

While there are similarities between Sartre's and Heidegger's thought, the latter presupposes in his work *What is Metaphysics?*[22] a much different experience, even though he does not describe it directly. Taking as a starting point the question raised by Leibniz—"Why is there any Being at all—why not rather Nothing?"[23] —Heidegger points out that feelings such as boredom, joy, and especially anguish in the face of nothingness[24] enable the revelation of an ongoing state: feeling in the midst of a what-is [or *Dasein*, being-there] that awakens wonder. Each mood characterizes an affective state in which is disclosed the what-is in its totality.[25] While Sartre's attitude is wholly negative, Heidegger's is both negative and positive: it includes admiration for the one who, when "called upon by the voice of being, experiences the wonder of all wonders: that beings *are*."[26] It thrives as a "response," a "sacrifice," a "thanking" before the mysterious "grace" by which Being is disclosed to human thought.[27] Ultimately, it requires a "protectiveness," namely "a care for our use of language."[28]

---

20. Sartre, *Nausea*, 127.
21. Sartre, *Nausea*, 131.
22. When referring to Heidegger's *What is Metaphysics?* the title also refers to two other Heidegger essays (an introduction and a postscript) sometimes joined to it and presented as a single text. Quotations from these texts are taken from Heidegger, *Pathmarks*, in which the three texts are presented as separate essays.
23. Heidegger, *Pathmarks*, 96; see 289.
24. A philosopher influenced by Heidegger pointed out the infiniteness that characterizes the experience of nothingness. See Welte, *Das Licht des Nichts*.
25. Heidegger, *Pathmarks*, 87.
26. Heidegger, *Pathmarks*, 234.
27. Heidegger, *Pathmarks*, 236.
28. Heidegger, *Pathmarks*, 237.

The Feeling of Transcendence, an Experience of God?

In considering the signals of transcendence described by Peter Berger,[29] namely, order, play, humor, hope, and damnation, these can be classified within the types I have identified. The need for order I would see as belonging to the second type—ontological. Moreover, Berger himself writes: "The argument from order is metaphysical rather than ethical."[30] When a mother comforts her child who has awakened frightened in the middle of the night, such an act "implies a statement about reality as such."[31] When she says to her child, "*Everything* is in order, *everything* is all right,"[32] her spontaneous words are not only affirming a particular order, but touch upon an order of the universe. While still unable to articulate the intellectual aspects of his or her feeling, the child finds total security, which exceeds the security of the present moment or of the family home.

Also of the second type are play and humor, since they, too, break through the boundaries of "reality." During activities such as children's games, board games, sports, music, stories, novels, theater, and liturgy, human beings carve out a time that is different from the ordinary time of everyday life and highlight the limits of ordinary time. Berger provides an example from his Austrian heritage when he mentions that just before Soviet troops occupied Vienna in 1945, the Vienna Philharmonic hardly missed a beat in its concert schedule. While fighting could be heard in the vicinity of the concert hall, the schedule was interrupted for only about a week, as if the orchestra insisted on the rights of beauty amid a war-ravaged country.

In the same way, humor challenges the seriousness of work and business. In the case of humor, as with play, human intelligence steps back from what the hubbub of daily life imposes as reality. And when a smile relates not to the minor failings of human beings but to the more tragic aspects of human life, it suggests that this tragic side may not have the last word.

29. Berger, *Rumor of Angels*, 65–90.
30. Berger, *Rumor of Angels*, 70.
31. Berger, *Rumor of Angels*, 68.
32. Berger, *Rumor of Angels*, 68.

Families of Mindsets

Hope and damnation belong to the third type—ethical. Hope offers an answer to the value of human existence: damnation, a revulsion before moral evil. When hope is desired for its own sake, it moves beyond the specific objects that are being pursued. Over and above the particular goods at stake, there is an affirmation of the pure and simple desire to live a worthy human life. Berger links hope to courage, reminiscent of Paul Tillich's "courage to be," which overcomes stoic resignation in the face of a reality that is seen as inherently limited.

Damnation, meanwhile, consists of a reflex of horror and rejection before any individual or group that harms the innocent: children, the elderly, the defenseless. A classic example of this banishment is that of Eichmann and other Nazis who cruelly humiliated, persecuted, and executed millions of people, mainly Jews. The reflex that not only wants to condemn such criminals but also to damn them for eternity is spontaneous and nearly universal. This reflex can be suspended briefly in the name of skepticism or scientific inquiry, or it can be overcome through forgiveness. However, such a reflex remains vital, at least in the first instances of a healthy moral response. It therefore should not be done away with, as it has much to say about the impact of our rejection of evil.

Lastly, the fourth type—interpersonal—is often found in the realm of theism, where belief in a personal God fosters a discourse inspired by human relations. It is found primarily in monotheistic religions, but also in Bhakti, a devotional movement within Hinduism that is rooted in love.[33] Within Christianity, attention is focused on Jesus, as various examples will soon show.

Each type or family of transcendent experience will now be illustrated with an example. An interesting challenge for the reader would be to try to identify in the four examples each of the six elements: preparation, occasion, feeling, discovery, reflection, and fruit. Following each account, I will suggest an analysis of these elements.

---

33. See Dhavamony, *Hindouisme*, 89–91.

The Feeling of Transcendence, an Experience of God?

A Case of Aesthetic Experience

This first account was written at my request by a student whom I will call Nicole, who granted me permission to use it. It belongs to the aesthetic type, given its occasion: the appearance of a large tree that has been struck by lightning.

> In the context of the transcendent experience, I like to remember something that may seem trivial but which for me is still the place where I felt, in I would say a tangible way, that my life was in the hands of an "Other." One evening, many years ago, a friend and I were walking down the street. We were heading for classes at the university. Clouds were gathering and the sky was growing darker, but we thought we would make it before the storm hit. We were wrong! We were only halfway there when suddenly thunder rumbled and a torrential downpour began. Lightning flashed over and over in a frightening rhythm. A good summer storm! As we recalled what we had been told as children, we agreed to change our usual route: it was lined with trees which, we thought, were perfect targets for lightning. We had just turned onto a side street when thunder shook the street we had just left. Even at a distance, the shaking was strong enough to throw us into the middle of the street, as if paralyzed and unable to react in any way . . . I remember that some people must have seen what was happening through their windows; they came out and asked us if we were all right and if we needed help . . . As it turns out, that evening we escaped with only a good scare, but we were shaken up enough that we decided to head back home.
>
> It is, however, the next day that indicated the deeper and more critical aspect of this event for me. Heading to the university along my usual route, I was able to see the devastation the lightning had caused. A giant maple tree that I had often admired as I walked by had been shattered; all that was left was the trunk and a few badly burned branches . . . I still cannot find words to express what I felt: the sight of it took my breath away! But a clear question came to me: What would I be, where would I be today if I had been standing in that spot last night

Families of Mindsets

– which was quite plausible? I clearly felt that a power greater than me had pulled me away ... the experience stayed with me for a long time ... my days and the things that made them up no longer had the same flavor ... I had grasped that they were leading me to a different place that was well beyond them, that Someone walked ahead of me, greeted me where I was and walked with me. Still today, I am filled with this conviction, which gives meaning to everything in my life.

Given that this was an unforeseeable event, we cannot speak of preparation as such. However, we can naturally assume the biological imperative of self-preservation within each human being. The occasion arises the day after the storm when Nicole, walking along her familiar route, could "see the devastation the lightning had caused." She is seized by a strong feeling: "the sight of it took my breath away." She suddenly discovers that she was nearly electrocuted, that she had been inches from leaving this world: "What would I be, where would I be today if I had been standing in that spot last night?" Her interpretation sticks closely to the actual event: "I clearly felt that a power greater than me had pulled me away." Lastly, the fruit is found in the "conviction" she has that "gives meaning to everything in my life," namely, that her days carried within them a transcendent dimension, "a different place that was well beyond them": that her existence was filled by "Someone."

A Case of Ontological Experience

Toward the end of his life, philosopher Jacques Maritain wrote: "A soul who is very close to me once gave me this testimony: 'It often happened that I experienced, through a sudden intuition, the reality of my being, of the profound, first principle which places me outside of nothingness. A powerful intuition, whose violence sometimes frightened me, and which has first given me the knowledge of a metaphysical absolute.'"[34] Ten years before that, he wrote

---

34. Maritain, *Peasant of the Garonne*, 111.

The Feeling of Transcendence, an Experience of God?

on the same issue in *Approaches to God*, from which the passage below is taken. In it, Maritain discusses this same intuition in a language influenced by Thomism and twentieth-century existentialism. This intuition turns out to be ontological: that is, it related to being.

> Before entering into the sphere of completely formed and articulated knowledge, in particular the sphere of metaphysical knowledge, the human mind is indeed capable of a prephilosophical knowledge which is virtually metaphysical. Therein is found the first, the primordial way of approach through which men become aware of the existence of God. . . .
>
> Let us rouse ourselves, let us stop living in dreams or in the magic of images and formulas, of words, of signs and practical symbols. Once a man has been awakened to the reality of existence and of his own existence, when he has really perceived that formidable, sometimes elating, sometimes sickening or maddening fact I exist, he is henceforth possessed by the intuition of being and the implications it bears with it.
>
> Precisely speaking, this primordial intuition is both the intuition of my existence and of the existence of things, but first and foremost of the existence of things. When it takes place, I suddenly realize that a given entity—man, mountain or tree—exists and exercises this sovereign activity to be in its own way, in an independence of me which is total, totally self-assertive and totally implacable.
>
> And at the same time I realize that I also exist, but as thrown back into my loneliness and frailty by this other existence by which things assert themselves and in which I have positively no part, to which I am exactly as naught. And no doubt, in face of my existence others have the same feeling of being frail and threatened. As for me, confronted with others, it is my own existence that I feel to be fragile and menaced, exposed to destruction and death. Thus the primordial intuition of being is the intuition of the solidity and inexorability of existence;

Families of Mindsets

and, second, of the death and nothingness to which my existence is liable.

And third, in the same flash of intuition, which is but my becoming aware of the intelligible value of being, I realize that this solid and inexorable existence, perceived in anything whatsoever, implies—I do not yet know in what form, perhaps in the things themselves, perhaps separately from them—some absolute, irrefragable existence, completely free from nothingness and death.

These three leaps—by which the intellect moves first to actual existence as asserting itself independently of me; and then from this sheer objective existence to my own threatened existence; and finally from my existence spoiled with nothingness to absolute existence—are achieved within the same unique intuition, which philosophers would explain as the intuitive perception of the essentially analogical content of the first concept, the concept of Being.

Next—this is the second stage—a prompt, spontaneous reasoning, as natural as this intuition (and as a matter of fact more or less involved in it), immediately springs forth as the necessary fruit of such a primordial apperception, and as enforced by and under its light. It is a reasoning without words, which cannot be expressed in articulate fashion without sacrificing its vital concentration and the rapidity with which it takes place. I see first that my being is liable to death; and second that it is dependent on the totality of nature, on the universal whole of which I am a part. I see that Being-with-nothingness, such as my own being, implies, in order that it should be, Being-without-nothingness—that absolute existence which I confusedly perceived from the beginning as involved in my primordial intuition of existence. But then the universal whole of which I am a part is itself Being-with-nothingness, by the very fact that I am part of it. And from this it follows finally that since this universal whole does not exist by virtue of itself, it must be that Being-without-nothingness exists apart from it. There is another Whole—a separate one—another Being, transcendent and self-sufficient and unknown in

The Feeling of Transcendence, an Experience of God?

itself and activating all beings, which is Being-without-nothingness, that is, self-subsisting Being, Being existing through itself.[35]

Unlike the first account, which described a one-time event, this narrative presents in a rather abstract fashion an intellectual experience that undoubtedly happens repeatedly. The author's use of the pronoun "I" is a clear sign of its existential nature. The preparation is found in his long philosophical reflection. The occasion is found in the first two intellectual leaps he describes: the awareness of the existence of things and of his own existence.

This awareness brings up intense feelings similar to those touched on by Sartre: in Maritain's words, "that formidable, sometimes elating, sometimes sickening or maddening fact *I exist*." He explains that the understanding of his own frailty comes from the relentless objectivity of other beings who strongly assert themselves: "As for me, confronted with others, it is my own existence that I feel to be fragile and menaced, exposed to destruction and death." He summarizes the first two intellectual leaps in this way: "Thus the primordial intuition of being is the intuition of the solidity and inexorability of existence; and, second, of the death and nothingness to which *my* existence is liable." Here Maritain and Heidegger have a similar outlook; both stress the negative aspect of the experience before presenting the positive aspect.

It is what Maritain refers to as the third leap that is his significant discovery: an openness to "some absolute, irrefragable existence, completely free from nothingness and death." As he points out at the beginning, we are dealing with a "prephilosophical knowledge which is *virtually metaphysical*." By "intuition" he means a Bergsonian understanding of the word that indicates a "primordial way of approach" that is taken "[b]efore entering into the sphere of completely formed and articulated knowledge."

Both forms of interpretation discussed in the previous chapter are present in Maritain's text. In the last paragraph, he presents the first form, the one inherent to the experience: "a

---

35. Maritain, *Approaches to God*, 3–6. I have subdivided one of the author's paragraphs to make it easier to identify the "three leaps" he describes.

prompt, spontaneous reasoning, as natural as this intuition (and as a matter of fact more or less involved in it), immediately springs forth." The foundation of his reasoning is not only the Being-with-nothingness of the individual, but, more broadly, the "universal whole" which also reveals itself as a Being-with-nothingness: "since this universal whole does not exist by virtue of itself, it must be that Being-without-nothingness exists apart from it."

Following this first form of interpretation, which we identified as a reflection *of* the experience—which in reality starts with a reflection *in* the experience—is a reflection *on* the experience. This second form grows out of this "completely formed and articulated knowledge" mentioned by Maritain at the beginning of his text. It is a question of metaphysics, practiced at its most technical level. Although it does not flow entirely from the transcendent experience (since it also draws on discursive sources), metaphysics is certainly its intellectual fruit.

A Case of Ethical Experience

The next account is by Madeleine Delbrêl. It belongs to the ethical type, since it presents a striking account of a great value: goodness.

> Nowadays it [goodness] has become almost something pejorative. No one wants to be a good girl anymore, or a good egg.... Who would want to devote his ambitions to a good work? Who recognizes the word "good" in "a good mess"? Is there anyone willing to bet that "good Christian" means the same thing as "saint"? Haven't we all heard the expression "goody-two-shoes"?
>
> And this deterioration of a word is almost always a sign that the reality it signifies has disappeared. Indeed, there is nothing rarer in our world than a good human being. In this same world, everything that has replaced goodness—solidarity, generosity, dedication—is accompanied in the various realms by a blind indifference to whole hosts of other human beings: in the economic realm, by an implacable cynicism; in the political realm, by cruelty; in the international realm, an enormous

The Feeling of Transcendence, an Experience of God?

disregard for the hunger of others, for the dying of others, for the physical or moral oppression of others. The hearts of those living in the modern world are slowly and imperceptibly suffocating from the universal absence of goodness.

Thus, coming into contact with a genuinely good man or a genuinely good woman causes in other people something that transcends the realm of thought, a veritable instance of the heart getting back its oxygen. These men and these women realize that they are getting back something that is essential to their human life. . . .

The goodness that I am talking about here is not having a good heart, being by nature someone with a good heart. But this goodness can turn a bad heart into a good heart. . . .

Through all of this, one thing remains the case: the proletariat will always show sympathy for anything that recalls goodness, genuine goodness, however much or little it may be. Yes, a genuine sympathy: they have a feel for it, they know what it means. In earlier aberrations, goodness—or at least a certain form of goodness—had little concern for justice. But now we have come to realize what dry bread justice is when it is not preceded by or completed with goodness. . . .

For a person to encounter the goodness of Christ in another person is in particular to encounter himself for what he really is. The world forces us to be ourselves plus something else: family, profession, nationality, race, class . . . . It necessarily groups us in series. It judges us according to what counts for the world as qualities and deficiencies, but does not touch who we really are. Each person in society feels himself branded by the original sins that vary according to the milieu and that are treated as incurable. But in relation to the goodness of Jesus Christ, it is the individual person who exists, and everything else is relativized in one fell swoop. . . .

I will most likely never know whether the woman about whom I'm going to speak was Christian or not.

I was in a big foreign city many years ago, coming to the last few hours of the several days I had spent there. I was almost entirely out of money, completely exhausted, and was suffering the pain that shakes the animal in the rational animal that we are: the pain of loss brought by death, by the several deaths of those who were of the same flesh as mine. I do not believe that I represented any social category. The clothes I was wearing had nothing particular about them.

I had been walking through the streets for several hours while I waited for my train. And why not say it? I was crying. But I didn't care anymore, and I waited for it to pass. A foreigner. A stranger. A sorrow that all people know, one that brings tears just as certain forms of work bring sweat.

It started to rain; I was hungry. The few coins remaining to me determined what I was permitted to eat. I went into a tiny café that also served food, and ordered what I could afford: some raw vegetables. I ate them slowly so that they would be more nourishing and also to give the rain a chance to stop. Every once in a while my eyes filled up with tears. Then, all of a sudden, a warm and comforting arm took me by the shoulders. A voice said to me: "You, coffee. Me, give." It was absolutely clear. I don't remember exactly what happened afterward, which is lucky for me because I don't much care for melodramatic scenes.

I have often spoken about this woman, thought about her, and prayed for her with an inexhaustible gratitude. When I look today for an example of goodness in flesh and bones, she is the one who comes to mind.

What makes this woman a Christian sign, a distant but faithful image of the goodness of God, is that she was good because goodness dwelled within her, and not because I was "one of her own," familially, socially, politically, nationally, or religiously. I was a "stranger" without any identifying marks. I was in need of goodness, and even that goodness that goes by the name of mercy. It was given me by that woman. Today she represents an absolute example of goodness because I was just "anybody," it didn't matter what or who I was, and because what she did for me she did simply because there was goodness in

The Feeling of Transcendence, an Experience of God?

her. In her simple gesture, I discovered everything that goodness has to be in order to be goodness."[36]

The more distant preparation in this account is Madeleine Delbrêl's concern for an often neglected, forgotten, or corrupted value: goodness. The near preparation seems to be the loss of family members; she mentions the "loss brought by death, by the several deaths of those who were of the same flesh as mine." A weary Madeleine finds herself in a foreign land, weeping in the rain. She enters a small café and, practically penniless, she does not order a meal, just raw vegetables. The critical occasion is the intervention of a woman who says to her: "You, coffee. Me, give." The woman's words and gesture stir up a feeling in Madeleine, apparently quite strong, of being comforted: "a warm and comforting arm took me by the shoulders."

The discovery is clearly that of the goodness embodied in this stranger. Delbrêl ends this passage by saying of this woman that "she represents an absolute example of goodness." Beyond the categories of social class or nationality, this comforting gesture makes Madeleine feel that she is recognized as a person, as an individual: "to encounter [oneself] for what [one] really is." The interpretation is provided through her reflections on the real meaning of goodness in today's world. Lastly, the fruit of the experience is, in addition to Madeleine's strengthened Christian commitment in a working-class milieu, a special relationship that endures with this stranger who comforted her that day: "I have often spoken about this woman, thought about her, and prayed for her with an inexhaustible gratitude."

A Case of Interpersonal Experience

A passage from a letter by Simone Weil—a Jewish philosopher with an interest in Ancient Greece—addressed to Father J.-M. Perrin, a Dominican friar, will illustrate the fourth and final type.

---

36. Delbrêl, *We, the Ordinary People*, 136–43.

Families of Mindsets

Until last September I had never once prayed in all my life, at least not in the literal sense of the word. I had never said any words to God, either out loud or mentally. I had never pronounced a liturgical prayer. I had occasionally recited the Salve Regina, but only as a beautiful poem.

Last summer, doing Greek with T . . . , I went through the 'Our Father' word for word in Greek. We promised each other to learn it by heart. I do not think he ever did so, but some weeks later, as I was turning over the pages of the Gospel, I said to myself that since I had promised to do this thing and it was good, I ought to do it. I did it. The infinite sweetness of this Greek text so took hold of me that for several days I could not stop myself from saying it over all the time. A week afterwards I began the vine-harvest. I recited the 'Our Father' in Greek every day before work, and I repeated it very often in the vineyard.

Since that time I have made a practice of saying it through once each morning with absolute attention. If during the recitation my attention wanders or goes to sleep, in the minutest degree, I begin again until I have once succeeded in going through it with absolutely pure attention. Sometimes it comes about that I say it again out of sheer pleasure, but I only do it if I really feel the impulse.

The effect of this practice is extraordinary and surprises me every time, for, although I experience it each day, it exceeds my expectation at each repetition.

At times the very first words tear my thoughts from my body and transport it to a place outside space where there is neither perspective nor point of view. The infinity of the ordinary expanses of perception is replaced by an infinity to the second or sometimes the third degree. At the same time, filling every part of this infinity of infinity, there is silence, a silence which is not an absence of sound but which is the object of a positive sensation, more positive than that of sound. Noises, if there are any, only reach me after crossing this silence.

Sometimes, also, during this recitation or at other moments, Christ is present with me in person, but his presence is infinitely more real, more moving, more clear

The Feeling of Transcendence, an Experience of God?

than on that first occasion when he took possession of me.

I should never have been able to take it upon myself to tell you all this had it not been for the fact that I am going away. And as I am going more or less with the idea of probable death, I do not believe that I have the right to keep it to myself. For after all, the whole of this matter is not a question concerning me myself. It concerns God. I am really nothing in it all. If one could imagine any possibility of error in God, I should think that it had all happened to me by mistake. But perhaps God likes to use cast-away objects, waste, rejects.[37]

Here the preparation for Simone Weil, who had never prayed formally, involves learning by heart the *Pater* in the original Greek of the New Testament. She is already a woman of great interiority who in all her activities nurtured concentration; the occasion of the experience is her decision to pray this prayer once every morning, with her full attention. As she comes to know this Greek text, she senses an "infinite sweetness" and she sometimes recites it "out of sheer pleasure." This feeling is sometimes accompanied by a sense of the presence of Christ, a "presence [that] is infinitely more real, more moving, more clear than on that first occasion when he took possession of me." This presence of Christ and the Father, whom she is addressing by reciting the *Pater*, allows us to consider her experience as interpersonal.

The transcendent discovery is related to spiritual infinity: "At times the very first words tear my thoughts from my body.... The infinity of the ordinary expanses of perception is replaced by an infinity to the second or sometimes the third degree." The fruit is twofold. On the one hand, a mystical consciousness is established, since the infinity within which Simone Weil sets herself is filled with a silence that allows her to embrace words and noises in a new way. On the other hand, as she mentions in the last paragraph of her account, her engagement in society remains intact and results in her intention during the Second World War to leave

---

37. Weil, *Waiting on God*, 23–24.

Families of Mindsets

England to join the French Resistance. But, already suffering from ill health, she would die before she could return home.

As we have seen, transcendent experiences can be classified into four main families of mindsets. Temperament and circumstances may lead a person to think they belong to one type rather than another. However, some serious thinkers have refused any such affiliation. In the next chapter, we will explore their reasons for rejecting transcendent experiences as illusory.

4

Rejections

So far, we have described, analyzed, and classified transcendent experiences in a way that has clearly acknowledged their importance but has also been purposely neutral with respect to whether they are true. It is now time to explore why not everyone accepts these experiences as transcendent, and to assess a number of critiques voiced against them.

The fact is that prominent thinkers have either completely denied such experiences or relativized their content or their importance. Some critiques are based on the self-sufficiency of the human person, either at the individual level or as a species participating in history; others, taking an opposite view, dispute the value of these accounts to better affirm the mystery of God and the purity of the act of faith. Lastly, since these are lived experiences, some psychologists have set themselves the task of charting the aftermath of such experiences to weigh the authenticity, judging the tree by the fruit it bears, as it were. It is therefore important to assess fairly these three standpoints that are suspicious of transcendent experiences.

In this chapter, I will examine positions of a philosopher and a psychoanalyst who reject these experiences in the name of an atheistic humanism, which wishes to affirm human reality by

Rejections

denying the existence of God. The next chapter will deal with the theological mistrust—the rejection of mysticism—voiced from within the Christian tradition by Karl Barth and his followers.

The discussion of these positions will be fairly brief to avoid bogging down our approach and lengthening this book. The cursory look we will take of these authors will obviously not allow us to discover all the subtleties of their work. It is still worth hearing them out and, in order to better appreciate them, understanding the cultural and intellectual contexts in which their rejections of religious experiences are formulated. The fundamental critiques that I will present, and the distance I will take with respect to their conclusions, do not prevent me from drawing on their search for clarity as a tool to assess the unequal value and the varying fruitfulness of the range of transcendent experiences.

Among those who have offered an unqualified rejection of the transcendent experience, I have chosen Feuerbach and Freud, both of whom have raised objections on the grounds of *projection*. Most readers will recognize this hurdle, or will have even raised the same objection, which certainly merits serious attention. Feuerbach's humanistic thought is found in his philosophical research and works, while Freud's similar stance comes from his work in the field of psychoanalysis.

Ludwig Feuerbach

Ludwig Feuerbach (1804–1872) is the first modern thinker to ground his atheism in both a humanist philosophical system and psychological considerations. Two great schools of thought—one philosophical, the other psychological—shaped his thinking and fueled his innovative work. In the philosophical arena, he draws on the pantheism of Spinoza and Hegel. Feuerbach develops a monism that is not centered on Nature (as with Spinoza) or on the Spirit (as in Hegel), but on Humanity. Reinforcing the influence of Spinoza and Hegel was the exegetical work of David Friedrich Strauss, who offers an interpretation of Jesus' deeds and words

The Feeling of Transcendence, an Experience of God?

that reduces them to an exclusively anthropological dimension.[1] In the field of psychology, Feuerbach draws on a long tradition of the psychological critique of religion that can be traced back to the Greeks and the Romans—Epicurus and Lucretius, in particular—and, as was the case with pantheism, influences Feuerbach through the works of Spinoza.[2]

Feuerbach's arguments are therefore grounded in philosophical and psychological considerations, which must be properly understood. I will first deal with his two philosophical arguments, which involve the infinite nature of humanity and how projection works.

The concept of the human species is central for Feuerbach. Unlike animals, human beings can grasp their own essential nature as an object of knowledge. Humans can objectify the characteristics of human nature, such as intellect, goodness, power, and so on. According to Feuerbach, such human attributes are limitless.

He considers as definitive Hegel's abolition of the ontological distinction between the divine and the human. However, he does not subscribe to the idea that, within absolute idealism, this distinction be eliminated for the benefit of the Spirit. In his view, it is not the absolute idea, but human sensibility and relationality, that make up the fabric of reality.

Here it is not only Hegel's influence at work, but also that of Strauss. The latter's aim is to bring out the *real* content—that is, the anthropological content—of the life of Jesus. On its own terms, Christology is displaced by philosophy by means of a radical reinterpretation in which humanity replaces God. In Strauss's view, what Christian dogma says of the man-God cannot be found in a single individual, even if that individual is Jesus, but must apply to humanity as a whole. Taking this intuition further, Feuerbach states that humanity reveals itself as fully divine in its consciousness of the human species through which we enjoy communion with one another.

---

1. See Xhaufflaire, *Feuerbach*, 191–216.
2. See Strauss, *Spinoza*, 45.

Rejections

His notion of human species[3] creates some confusion, because it combines a logical element and a factual element. The term "human species" refers both to an abstract idea, comprising general characteristics, and to a concrete reality, namely all humankind. In the case of the former, ideally or theoretically, humanity has unlimited attributes, since they can potentially be reproduced and enhanced *ad infinitum*. In the case of the latter, however, humanity consists of a group of finite beings, no matter how large their number. It is easy to confuse something that is quantitatively infinite (indefinite growth) with something qualitatively or ontologically infinite (namely, the absolutely perfect being). Even if the growth of the human population increased constantly, exponentially, an aggregate of more and more finite beings would never result in a qualitative infinite. Clearly, Feuerbach failed to prove his starting premise: that humanity was qualitatively infinite, that is, divine.

Still from a philosophical perspective, the thesis of the infinite nature of humanity goes hand in hand with a second thesis, which aims to explain why religious people reject this claim of the infinite nature of humanity. This is the famous thesis of projection, which suggests that essentially human traits are projected onto God. According to Feuerbach, the believer is seriously mistaken when attributing these traits to God. In doing so, the believer renounces values that are in fact their own and transfers them to God. All that the believer admires in God is, in reality, but a reflection, as if in a mirror, of humanity's intrinsic nature. Religion thus diminishes humanity by enhancing God with traits that belong to humankind.

In this context, Feuerbach suggests that Christianity is both the most human and the most inhuman of religions. The most human because of the Incarnation and the person of Jesus; but also the most inhuman because it highlights the contrast between God and humanity. Feuerbach's main concern is to do away with this contrast, which exalts God while diminishing humankind. Thus, he endorses Schleiermacher in defining piety as feeling:

---

3. Author's note: The German word *Gattung* can mean both "genus" and "species." Here I have chosen to use "species."

The Feeling of Transcendence, an Experience of God?

Feuerbach praises Schleiermacher, the last of the Christian theologians, for having founded a religion based on the anthropologically rich concept of feeling. He, however, blames Schleiermacher for not having drawn the implications of such a perspective, namely that God is nothing more than the essence of feeling.[4]

What can be said about projection? For one, that before being projected—as an illusion or not—such human qualities must first be observed in actual, visible people. But if such traits exist in a finite state in human beings, how is this in contradiction with their residing in God in an infinite state? Moreover, if the idea of creation allows us to see in God the foundation of these human riches, how can this take away from their reality? In other words, far from diminishing human beings by depriving them of their qualities, does not the greatness of God affirm them by giving them a source and a meaning?

Since Feuerbach, "projection" has been seen as a negative term. However, projection is only an error if it *presupposes* that God does not exist and that humanity is divine. A more fruitful intellectual path is found if the word "projection" is seen as neutral, such that it is therefore possible to state without difficulty that religion necessarily entails a mode of projection. The problem now becomes one of distinguishing, in each particular case, healthy and unhealthy projection. Healthy projection does not diminish humankind by recognizing that something exists in a state of perfection in God, while unhealthy projection does diminish human experience, as demonstrated by Feuerbach's diagnosis, which will be completed by Freud.

In turning to Feuerbach's psychological critique, I must complete the list of shortcomings he identifies in Christianity. In his view, not only does it eliminate human values to hand them over to God, but Christ's religion is shown to be antisocial. It prevents the individual from contributing to the betterment of the

---

4. Xhaufflaire, *Feuerbach*, 170 (translation from Xhaufflaire's French). The author refers to the first edition of Feuerbach's complete works in German (Feuerbach, *Sämtliche Werke*, vol. 1, 249).

Rejections

human species by focusing the individual on the issue of their personal salvation. It holds in contempt the world, sexuality, work, and culture. It fosters individuality by enjoining the believer to fall back on their subjectivity and to seek their ultimate happiness there. In this way, Christianity turns individuals away from both nature and other people, preventing the forming of productive relationships with them.

This alienation from the true infinite that is humanity would also stem from the fundamental passivity inherent in religious experience. Religiosity is born of a feeling of helplessness and dependence with respect to nature: a dependence from which humanity has attempted to free itself through the illusion that it shares in God's almighty power and immortality. Religion is thus but an attempt by the human being to fulfill its longing for happiness by taking refuge in artificial feelings, especially the feeling of being freed from the tribulations of its bodily existence. Feuerbach writes that "desire constitutes the source, the essence itself of religion."[5] It is an irrational desire which belies reality and tries to escape it.

A possible response would be that the religion he rejects is not representative of Christianity. However, Feuerbach clearly distinguishes nineteenth-century Christianity—that of Schleiermacher, for example, a strongly anthropocentric one—from classic Christianity, which is his direct target. The Christian authors that he cites most often are not those on the fringes, but leading figures such as Tertullian, Origen, Jerome, Augustine, Luther, and Calvin. In fact, the opposition Feuerbach raises between the human and the divine, nature and the supernatural can be found in the work of many of those theologians—an opposition that is found neither in the Greek Fathers nor in Thomas Aquinas, who are just as much classic Christian thinkers as the aforementioned ones.

Feuerbach is therefore denouncing a type of Christianity—fairly widespread, especially since Luther—that suggests that God's riches and power go hand in hand with humankind's poverty and

---

5. Quoted in Xhaufflaire, *Feuerbach*, 253 (translation from Xhaufflaire's French). (Feuerbach, *Sämtliche Werke*, vol. 1, 443.)

The Feeling of Transcendence, an Experience of God?

helplessness. In this respect, this critique has been and can still be beneficial, since it challenges believers to examine the motive for their faith and ask themselves if, in certain ways, it makes their life poorer rather than richer.

Underlying his psychological critique of religion, Feuerbach seems to take for granted that any object that goes beyond human capacities is illusory. Thus, he condemns the desire for total happiness, for immortality, for a spiritual protection against anything that threatens human life—physically, morally, or ontologically. The problematic issue here is the universal nature of his condemnation. On the one hand, if religious desire brings about or justifies indifference and irresponsibility toward others, then the desire is clearly pathological and Feuerbach's critique should serve as a warning to be heeded. In this case, this poorly grounded desire fosters the emergence of a religious thought which is also at odds with reality.

On the other hand, an object, whether finite or infinite, that a person might ardently wish to exist, may actually exist as not exist. The person's desire for its existence is neither proof nor disproof that it exists. In itself, desire is unable to indicate whether something is real or imaginary. For example, two individuals can be involved in a true collaboration which can produce observable results, regardless of the good or bad desires that either one of them may want to satisfy, more or less consciously, through this relationship.

We can conclude that, although Feuerbach's philosophical arguments regarding the infinite nature of humanity and the intellectual mode of projection do not prove what they are trying to prove, his psychological critique is not without merit. While it does not refute the actual object of religion, its significance is undeniable when it comes to skewed forms of religion. I will discuss this crucial issue in chapters 6 and 7. For now, we will explore how, starting from the same general viewpoint as Feuerbach, Freud goes further still in the analysis of the aberrations of religion.[6]

6. The link between Freud and Feuerbach is suggested in a section devoted to Freud in Küng, *Does God Exist?*, 262–323. Küng gives a good presentation

Rejections

Sigmund Freud

Like Feuerbach, Freud (1856-1939) believes that religion is illusory and supports this view with a series of philosophical and psychological arguments.[7]

His philosophical argument is rather rudimentary compared to Feuerbach's. The latter belonged to the great era of German Idealist thought, ending around 1850, while Freud's intellectual world is marked by the positivism of the end of the nineteenth century. In chapter 7 of *The Future of an Illusion*,[8] he states that his views against religion do not require the support of psychoanalysis. He recognizes that such views were known well before the advent of psychoanalysis. However, he defends the novelty of his views on the grounds that they add a certain psychological basis to the critiques formulated by his illustrious predecessors.

Before turning to explore in more detail Freud's psychological basis, which is indeed his original contribution to the debate, let us look briefly at the philosophical argument he borrows from those who came before him. It is not an argument that has often been disputed on its own merits, undoubtedly due to the fact that it pales in comparison to Freud's brilliant psychoanalytic discoveries. Many commentators have overlooked the weakness of his philosophical position, preferring to focus on the clearly fascinating aspects of the unconsciousness of religiosity.[9] What we don't

---

of Freud's ideas, mainly on religion, in the context of his biography, different aspects of Austrian culture, and scientific thought (e.g., biological, medical, and ethnological) of the period. The link between Feuerbach and Freud had already been suggested, albeit on a minor point, in Jones, *Last Phase*, vol. 3, 385-86, where the author quotes H. B. Acton.

7. The following authors shed light on Freud's atheism by introducing his personality, biography, and historical context: Dempsey, *Freud, Psychoanalysis, Catholicism*, 25-55; Plé, *Freud et la religion*, 43-71; Zilboorg, *Psychoanalysis and Religion*, 195-243 (with significant corrections to the interpretations of Freud's atheism provided by his famous biographer, Ernest Jones).

8. Freud, "Future of an Illusion."

9. For example, in Ricoeur, *Freud and Philosophy*, 233-34, the author simply mentions the rationalism and scientism of Freud's time and milieu without in any way speaking of the ramifications with respect to the validity of his

The Feeling of Transcendence, an Experience of God?

tend to see is that some of the conclusions drawn from the analysis of psychological mechanisms are grounded in inadequate philosophical foundations.

In chapter 7 of *The Future of an Illusion*, Freud adopts the principle that science is the only way that can lead to knowledge of reality. This premise goes hand in hand with his proposed distinction between error and illusion. A person commits an error independently of their desires, while an illusion is closely linked to such desires. An error can be corrected through logical or empirical refutation, while an illusion can be neither proven nor refuted. An illusion is a psychologically motivated belief that has no intellectual value. Religious ideas belong to the realm of the illusory since they correspond to the most fervent desires of humanity.

Freud claims that his definition of religion as an illusion is strictly psychological; however, this is not the case. While he states at the beginning of chapter 6 of *The Future of an Illusion* that he will use a scientifically *neutral* notion of "illusion," it is apparent that in chapters 8 and 9 he has reverted to its more familiar *negative* connotation. In chapter 6 he maintains that an illusion cannot be refuted; but in chapter 8, he states that religion "comprises a system of wishful illusions together with a *disavowal of reality*."[10]

Progressing through the book, we observe a major semantic shift. Can this simply be attributed to an "error" on Freud's part? Similarly, in chapter 9, he points out that "[w]hen a man has once brought himself to accept uncritically all the absurdities that religious doctrines put before him and even to overlook the contradictions between them, we need not be greatly surprised at the weakness of his intellect."[11]

In doing so, on the philosophical level, independent of his analysis of psychological mechanisms, the die is cast for Freud: he has opted for a reductionist definition of "reality." His positivist philosophy can admit only earthly life as reality: "Freud was a sceptical and resigned man (especially in the period after the First

---

critique of religion.

10. Freud, "Future of an Illusion," 43 (italics mine).
11. Freud, "Future of an Illusion," 48.

Rejections

World War); he was the last great man of the Enlightenment...."[12] His stoic outlook makes him deeply suspicious of anything in human desire that goes beyond the limits of reality as determined by positivism. When the pleasure principle gives way to the reality principle, a person experiences an urge toward two subjectively incompatible actions, and not because the person is interested in this reality itself by virtue of a desire that has the reality as its goal.[13]

Indeed, for Freud, the human being is essentially biological and psychological, not intentional. Higher-order human experiences have no coherence in and of themselves, but are at best a sublimation of lesser tendencies.[14] In this way, science, art, and love have value in Freud's eyes. But religion does not rank: while science, art, and love allow people to have access to a higher-order pleasure, religion remains necessarily infantile.[15]

It is important to point out that Freud does not speak as a scientist when he affirms that science is the only path to a legitimate knowledge of reality. This statement is meta-scientific; it comes from philosophy.[16] More specifically, any judgment about the purview of science is the result of a human mind reflecting on its scientific activity. Such self-understanding is of little import to Freud. His position reflects a philosophy that pays no attention to the experience a person may have of their intentionality—that is to say, of their capacity to tend toward truth, an experience as fundamental as a person's biological and psychological life. Based on whether or not one has unblocked the features of this experience, a

---

12. Fromm, "Post-Marxian and Post-Freudian," 148.

13. In opposition to Aristotle, for example, Freud suggests that a child's endless questions indicate a desire to know that is always serving hidden interests. See Freud, "Leonardo da Vinci," 78–79.

14. Roland Dalbiez notes a theoretical wavering of Freud regarding sublimation. On the one hand, Freud is inclined toward a radical empiricism: the activity of the higher psyche is of the same nature as sexual energy. On the other hand, when speaking of science and art as taking in elements borrowed from instincts, he admits that art and science possess their own specific qualities. See Dalbiez, *Psychoanalytical Method*, vol. 1, 375–77, 383; vol. 2, 289–93.

15. See Plé, *Freud et la religion*, 121–22.

16. See Dalbiez, *Psychoanalytical Method*, vol. 2, 280–83.

The Feeling of Transcendence, an Experience of God?

person will propose a vision of the human being that is either fully integrated or reductionist.

Let us now turn to Freud's psychological argument against religious experience. It builds on the argument proposed by Feuerbach, who highlights the role played by two primordial feelings: fear before the threat posed by nature, and the need for some compensatory protection. To these elements, Freud will add an in-depth analysis of the psychological mechanisms at play in the illusion that religion is thought to be.

For Freud, religion is essentially a relationship to God the Father. In *Totem and Taboo*, Freud writes:

> The psychoanalysis of individual human beings, however, teaches us with quite special insistence that the god of each of them is formed in the likeness of his father, that his personal relation to God depends on his relation to his father in the flesh and oscillates and changes along with that relation, and that at bottom God is nothing other than an exalted father.[17]

It must be noted that the discovery expressed here includes an absolutist "is nothing other than," which fails to take into account other factors that will be discussed in chapters 6 and 7. That being said, Freud's statement, which will later be nuanced by other psychologists, remains valid. Aware of his or her own limitations, and in turn impressed and disappointed by his or her father's limited power, the child creates for itself the image of any omnipotent invisible Father, with whose almighty power it hopes to be reconciled.

This relation to the Father is, however, not a harmonious one. It is characterized by an ambivalence of two opposing emotions, one of which—hate—remains in the unconscious. Guilt-ridden sons struggle with their hostile feelings toward the Father by creating prohibitions and performing rituals designed to ensure his benevolence. The fact that an obsessive recurrence of these prohibitions and rituals has been observed leads to a view

---

17. Freud, "Totem and Taboo," 147.

that religion must be, at the collective level, a phenomenon similar to the obsessive-compulsive disorder that we see at the individual level.

In *The Future of an Illusion*, Freud specifies the three functions performed by this compensatory religion: it provides security for humankind in the face of nature, allows humankind to come to terms with destiny and death, and helps deal with the inhibitions arising from social life. Thus, Freud affirms a purely functional view of religion, whereas science, which is destined to replace it, is for him both functional and true. As functional, science—and especially psychoanalysis—will assist human beings to know themselves and deal with their problems. As true, it will allow human beings to live in a lucid way and to accept their limits.

In *Civilization and Its Discontents*,[18] Freud returns to these ideas. At the beginning of this essay, he rejects the idea that the "oceanic feeling" is a strictly religious phenomenon. He falls back on his definition of religion as relation to the Father. Since the oceanic feeling is, in my opinion, clearly a type of transcendent experience, I will postpone discussion of it until chapter 6, so I can report on it with the help of other psychologists.

In this same essay, Freud claims that religion is nothing but a collective delusion. Dalbiez notes two points regarding this claim. On the one hand, there is a noticeable and frequent correlation between the presence of sexual themes and the presence of religious content when it comes to delusion. On the other hand, in the strict sense of the term, delusion is associated with the insane who, suffering from unsociability, are profoundly alone in their delusion; or, if the delusion is induced, it affects at most two or three people, most often members of the same family, but not large groups. It is therefore difficult to rightly speak of religion as a delusion that would affect an entire community.[19]

Freud's critique of religion is partly based on a parallel he draws between clinical observations of individuals and collective religious phenomena. Many ethnologists have challenged the

---

18. Freud, "Civilization," 63–74.
19. Dalbiez, *Psychoanalytical Method*, vol. 2, 314–19.

The Feeling of Transcendence, an Experience of God?

validity of this parallel. Anthropologist Evans-Pritchard's review of Freud's ethnological hypotheses demonstrates the shortcomings of these theories, which Evans-Pritchard sees as "emotionalist" and "evolutive." He also dismisses the idea that one can move from ontogeny (the individual level, studied psychologically) to phylogeny (the collective level, which must be addressed as a cultural system).[20]

In conclusion, Freud's insistence on the father figure in religion is extremely worthwhile, as is his analysis of the psychological mechanisms that bring this role to life. I will return to the father figure and these mechanisms in chapter 6.

However, we must state that his rejection of the truth of religious beliefs is unfounded, philosophically speaking. As was the case for Feuerbach, the problems that concern Freud present a twofold challenge: intellectual and psychic. Only philosophy can deal with the first aspect, which explains why psychologists remain divided on this issue. Freud himself was perceptive enough to predict that other members of his profession would use psychoanalytical grounds to counter his antireligious arguments.[21] He did not foresee, however, the drastic change that, after his death, would transform the psychoanalytic method toward the phenomenon of religion. This will form a part of the discussion in chapter 6.

---

20. Evans-Pritchard, *Primitive Religion*, chapter 2 and conclusion.
21. Freud, "Future of an Illusion," 36–37.

5

A Prophetic Denunciation?

Like Feuerbach and Freud, the renowned Swiss Protestant theologian Karl Barth (1886–1968) and his admirers have little, if anything, good to say about transcendent experiences. However, their reasons are completely different from those discussed in the previous chapter. Rather than arming himself with philosophical and psychological weapons, Barth uses theological ones. Indeed, he extols the Christian *faith*, based on God's grace, but condemns *religion* as the dogged will of self-aggrandizement, based on a person's own powers, including on the spiritual level.

That being said, it is important to consider whether Barth's views were not more open and nuanced than those of some of his disciples, who viewed transcendent experiences as worthless religious phenomena in terms of faith. Theologians—both Protestant and Catholic—who have made more rigid the faith/religion dualism have imparted a mistrust of mysticism to large segments of the Christian churches. An example of this is found in the work of Emil Brunner, who mounts an all-guns-blazing attack on Schleiermacher in his book *Mystik und das Wort* [Mysticism and the Word][1]—an attack from which Barth would distance himself

---

1. Brunner, *Die Mystik*. However, in Benz, *Mystical Sources*, 103, n. 3, the author argues that later Brunner changed his mind: "To be convinced of the

The Feeling of Transcendence, an Experience of God?

early in his career.² The division between mysticism and biblical religion is also expressed, in rather extreme terms, in the work of Reinhold Niebuhr.³ When this dogmatic mistrust toward mysticism joins forces with the traditional mistrust of psychoanalysis toward the religious phenomenon, the result is a well-rationalized closed-mindedness to transcendent experiences.⁴

Starting in 1911, when he became pastor in Safenwil, Switzerland, Barth started to notice and then examine the weaknesses of Christian thought of the modern era.⁵ He particularly questioned the emphasis that Christian thought places on experience, at the expense of obedient attentiveness to the Word of God. In this respect, one could expect him to reject transcendent experience as incompatible with such obedient attentiveness to God's Word.

As we will soon see, things are not so clear cut. Barth offers three kinds of writings that are germane to this question. First, historical reflections aimed at explaining the emergence of the Feuerbach phenomenon within the Lutheran world. Next, well-known writings in which his antithesis between faith and religion emerges; the mystical experience, which stems from religion, has no validity. Finally, in his later writings, a return to the question with a different outlook that provides an obviously favorable view of what he calls "true"⁶ human words coming from non-biblical contexts.

---

legitimacy of Christian mysticism, he had to spend two years in Japan and encounter the Japanese mysticism represented by Uchimura, founder of the no-church-movement (mu-kyo-kai)."

2. Barth, "Brunners Schleiermacherbuch," in which the author holds it was not to mysticism that Schleiermacher gave way, but rather to nineteenth-century "Kulturreligion" in its exaltation of work—salvation by works (56–58).

3. Niebuhr, *Nature and Destiny*, vol. 1, 135–36.

4. An illustration of this is found in the work of psychologist-theologian Godin, *Psychological Dynamics*.

5. See Leuba, *Études barthiennes*, 54–60.

6. Barth, *CD*, vol. 27, IV.3.1, §69, 110. All quotations and references will be to this 2009 Study Edition of Barth's work. However, following the publisher's note in vol. 1, vi, page references will be to the classic 14-volume set (1936–1977), as the classic edition page numbers are found in the margins of the 2009 edition.

A Prophetic Denunciation?

We will explore each of these three kinds of texts in turn. In doing so, we will take care to bring to light, in these changes in viewpoint, the cohesiveness of Barth's thought as well as his cautious opening up to the idea that transcendent experiences can play a positive role within theology.

Historical Considerations

Many passages from Barth offer a critical reading of the anthropologizing trend that, in his view, characterizes modern history. In a section of his *Church Dogmatics* that deals with the two natures of Christ, he provides an excursus where he traces this trend to a christological doctrine of the young Luther. This doctrine is that of the divinization of the humanity of Christ stemming from its intimate association with the divine. Barth suggests that within Lutheran circles, which were unfortunately unwilling to accept the Calvinist critique of this doctrine, the way was open to a development of this doctrine within German idealism, where it became the apotheosis of human nature. He makes it clear that they unwittingly opened the door that led, in his view, to the great heresy of the nineteenth century: the exaltation of the human being at God's expense. It is certainly possible to see a link between the Lutheran glorification of the humanity of Christ and the philosophical glorification that posits "the divinity of humanity as a whole and as such."[7]

In Barth's view, Feuerbach's thinking is the outcome of this secularized Lutheran thought. Barth refers to Feuerbach in this same passage from *Church Dogmatics* when he observes that Feuerbach "usually liked to appeal to Luther for his theory of the identity of divine with human essence."[8] Feuerbach is the subject of a full chapter in Barth's great work on nineteenth-century German theology.[9] The chapter shows an obvious sympathy for the person

---

7. Barth, *CD*, vol. 24, IV/2/1, §64, 82; see 80–83.
8. Barth, *CD*, vol. 24, IV/2/1, §64, 83.
9. Barth, *Protestant Theology*, 534–40.

The Feeling of Transcendence, an Experience of God?

of Feuerbach, whom Barth considers a theologizing philosopher: that is to say, a man who did nothing but theology—in his own way, of course!—in passionately promoting atheism. The key point to notice here is that Feuerbach's understanding of the human being is not out of place when set within a historical process from Luther to Schleiermacher. Yet, Barth presents the inner logic of this process as an estrangement from the living God through the acceptance of an increasingly comprehensive anthropocentrism.

A First Set of Writings

In his *Church Dogmatics*, Barth offers two sets of writings dealing with religion: the first is found in volume I (to which I will add a passage from volume II), and the second is in volume IV. A period of just over twenty-five years separates the two: the first volume was published in German in 1932, and the fourth in 1959. To refer to them as two sets of writings underlines the continuity between them, because to speak in terms of two antithetical positions would suggest too much of a difference in their content. Even though they offer distinct contributions to the conversation, they are interconnected.[10]

In the first set of writings, entitled "The Word of God and Experience,"[11] Barth puts forth the following proposition: an "experience [*Erfahrung*] of the Word of God" is given to human beings; from this comes a knowledge that determines their existence. Fidelity to the Bible excludes any attempt to self-appropriate one's experience as a pious or mystical realm that would belong to the human being. Just before this section, Barth rejects the idea, attributed to Schleiermacher, that the encounter between humankind

---

10. Contrary to Hans Küng (see Küng, *Does God Exist?*, 514–18 and 525–27), I do not believe that Barth fundamentally changed his position. In opposition to the position taken by three authors who propose a radical change, Francis Schüssler Fiorenza emphasizes the continuity in Barth's thought; with respect to the presuppositions of his reply to Feuerbach, see Schüssler Fiorenza, "Responses of Barth," 149–66; especially 151–55.

11. Barth, *CD*, vol. 1, I/1/1, §6.3, 198–227.

A Prophetic Denunciation?

and God must be understood as the actualization of an instance of religious potential that could be explored in general.[12]

Also as part of this first set of writings from volume I of *Church Dogmatics*, there is a section entitled "The Revelation of God as the Abolition of Religion."[13] In it, Barth presents the distinction he draws between Christian revelation and religion. By religion or religious consciousness he means the fundamental inclination within the human being to decide on its attitude toward the mystery. Because it emanates from the human being, this attitude is opposed to God's revelation. It consists in humans' belief in their own thoughts and their trust in the justice of their works. It is therefore an ersatz consciousness which counters divine intervention. It is equal to a shutting down: religion cannot be seen as "a kind of outstretched hand which is filled by God in His revelation." Barth calls it a "mistaken faith," an "unbelief" that leads only to "a complete fiction, which has not only little but no relation to God."[14]

Near the mid-point of this long argument, Barth is not gentle in his view of mysticism: namely, the religiosity that overlooks outward forms and interprets Christian traditions in its own way, building on them to feed on them. The problem he sees with mysticism is that it denies the explicit content of dogma without admitting that it contradicts these dogmas, claiming to discern their "true" meaning, such as when it identifies God with the secret identity of the human ego.[15]

Barth returns to this question in a later volume,[16] in which he expresses his disagreement with the passage in *Confessions* (IX, 10) where St. Augustine recounts the mystical experience he had with his mother, Monica. Using the same words that Augustine uses in his description, Barth sees in this experience "the consequence of an *ascendere* and *transcendere* of all the limitations

---

12. Barth, *CD*, vol. 1, I/1/1, §6.2, 192–93.
13. Barth, *CD*, vol. 4, I/2/2, §17, 280–361.
14. Barth, *CD*, vol. 4, I/2/2, §17, 303.
15. Barth, *CD*, vol. 4, I/2/2, §17, 319.
16. Barth, *CD*, vol. 7, II/1/1, §25, 10–12.

The Feeling of Transcendence, an Experience of God?

and restrictions of man's existence and situation." He states that in this ascent and transcendence, "we wilfully hurry past God, who descends in His revelation into this world of ours."[17] The divine descent of the Incarnation rules out any human ascent. Barth also wants to denounce the notion that access to God would consist of identification with the divine. He stresses that the relation between the human being and God involves a distinction between the two—a theme to which he returns a little later.[18]

Barth takes up his critique of mysticism in another context, where he puts forth the following proposition: on the one hand, "the impossibility of the [human] attempt to speak of God" (apophatic philosophy);[19] on the other hand, God "can make possible for man that which is not possible for him of himself."[20] God, however, makes this possible only in the official proclamation of the church. Only those who hear the Word of God and strive to pass it on faithfully are beneficiaries of "a divine victory concealed in human failure.... God then makes good what we do badly...," thus making efficacious something that is completely beyond human power. It is from this perspective of grace that the apophatic belief gets its meaning: "That man really cannot really speak of God is only realised when it is known that he really can really speak of God."[21] Thus, Barth emphatically states:

> The mystic and the agnostic philosopher apparently use the same phrases. They speak of God and they say the same things about Him in what seem to be very much the same language: that it is not possible for us to speak of Him. But by God they do not mean the Creator of Heaven and Earth, the Lord and Judge and Saviour of Man.[22]

---

17. Barth, *CD*, vol. 7, II/1/1, §25, 11.
18. Barth, *CD*, vol. 7, II/1/1, §25, 56–57.
19. Barth, *CD*, vol. 6, I/2/3, §22, 750.
20. Barth, *CD*, vol. 6, I/2/3, §22, 751.
21. Barth, *CD*, vol. 6, I/2/3, §22, 751.
22. Barth, *CD*, vol. 6, I/2/3, §22, 750.

A Prophetic Denunciation?

Indeed, to realize that one knows nothing about God, a divine word must come before the stage of negation in order to have a basis for the negation.

So far, it may seem that Barth is praising Christianity to the detriment of other religions. This is not at all the case. Indeed, as Barth sees it, even Christianity, *as religion*, "is still human religion and therefore unbelief, like all other religions."[23] As an observable phenomenon, Christianity also falls under divine judgment. Furthermore, if it accepts revelation, any religion can become in some way true: on the condition, in short, that it becomes Christian. Therefore, as we can see, when all is said and done, only Christianity can be true. But its truth, like its validity, remains extrinsic in relation to the truth of God.[24]

A Later Contribution

More recent considerations by Barth on this topic offer a new perspective.[25] Eschewing the revelation/religion dialectic that marked his first writings, he turns to the relationship between the Word of God and true human words. The change in viewpoint does not represent a contradiction, since Barth's underlying theology remains unchanged. In fact, this second point of view shows the surprising possibilities offered by this underlying theology.

Barth begins by recognizing that outside the Bible and the church there "are . . . other words which are quite notable in their own way, other lights which are quite clear and other revelations which are quite real."[26] They are "words of great seriousness, profound comfort and supreme wisdom" which, in their own way,

---

23. Barth, *CD*, vol. 4, I/2/2, §17, 353.

24. In order to keep this chapter to a reasonable length, I have limited my references to *Church Dogmatics*. It is well known that Barth's wide offensive against "religion" and therefore mysticism can be traced to the second edition (1922) of Barth, *Epistle to the Romans*, in particular, 28, 44–51, 109–10, 149–50; note, however, page 79, on the expectation of the pagans.

25. Barth, *CD*, vol. 27, IV/3/1, §69.2, especially 96–165.

26. Barth, *CD*, vol. 27, IV/3/1, §69.2, 97.

The Feeling of Transcendence, an Experience of God?

also come from the Creator, since they are "words which are illuminating and helpful to the degree that God Himself gives it to them to be illuminating and helpful as such words."[27] True to his theological outlook, Barth does not consider these words as equal to, and even less as superior to, the Word of God. There is no need to rely on "an original truth superior both to the truth of the world and to that of God."[28] It is, on the contrary, the truth of God that is the measure of all the others. Thus, human words must be evaluated by the yardstick of revelation.[29]

Throughout the enigmatic and mysterious cosmos, and in spite of the perverted relationship between humanity and its Creator, God has shone a light.[30] Associated with the epiphany of Jesus Christ, the cosmos also speaks. Barth goes so far as to write that the "truth given it by God in and with its actuality endures."[31] However, it is the Word of God proclaimed in the narrower confines of the Bible and the church that authenticate the words gathered from the cosmos.[32] God's truth both problematizes and relativizes the truth of the cosmos, but it also establishes it by integrating it within a horizon of creation and covenant.[33] In concrete terms, the non-biblical word will be fruitful if, far from pacifying and reassuring, it communicates a "true call to repentance."[34]

Many interpreters of Barth's thought have drawn out the major implications of volume IV/3 of his *Church Dogmatics*. Elizabeth J. Lacelle, for example, notes that it is Barth's interest in the cosmic word that allows him to extend his famous *analogia fidei* to an *analogia historiae*. This in turns leads to Barth's theology of the Holy Spirit, awakener to the living relationship between the

---

27. Barth, *CD*, vol. 27, IV/3/1, §69.2, 97.
28. Barth, *CD*, vol. 27, IV/3/1, §69.2, 152.
29. Barth, *CD*, vol. 27, IV/3/1, §69.2, 110–11.
30. Barth, *CD*, vol. 27, IV/3/1, §69.2, 138–39.
31. Barth, *CD*, vol. 27, IV/3/1, §69.2, 139.
32. Barth, *CD*, vol. 27, IV/3/1, §69.2, 115.
33. Barth, *CD*, vol. 27, IV/3/1, §69.2, 153–54, 163–64.
34. Barth, *CD*, vol. 27, IV/3/1, §69.2, 129.

A Prophetic Denunciation?

human being and God in history.³⁵ Alice Collins also highlights the importance of this theology of the Holy Spirit. The presence of the Spirit indeed makes possible some form of legitimate anthropocentrism within Barth's theological construct. Thus, to God's initiative toward the human being—movement from the top down—is added, through the Holy Spirit, the human being's search for God—movement from the bottom up. In this way, Barth is finally able to address the anthropological concerns of liberal theology without setting aside his own theological vision, which always has as its starting point biblical revelation.³⁶

A Suspicion in Need of Interpretation

With Barth, the religious phenomenon is usually devalued in relation to the Word of God. He does not tend to deal with experiences and discoveries that, having taken place before the proclamation of the Word of God and justification, might together also form part of God's gifts—prevenient graces—and an initial human response. In his book on St. Anselm, Barth does, however, recognize that the spiritual quest is a gift from God: "all right seeking (it is also grace) would be of no avail if God did not 'show' himself, if the encounter with him were not in fact primarily a movement from his side and if the finding that goes with it . . . did not take place."³⁷ However, here Barth denies any validity to a quest that does not lead to an explicitly Christian revelation. He does not ask himself whether there is room for transcendent experiences as calls from God that would lead to meaningful personal growth without the process necessarily leading to an act of faith in Jesus Christ.

It is, however, possible to glean from the writings of Barth that we have examined a few answers to our initial question about transcendent experiences. First, Barth does make room for

---

35. Lacelle, "Karl Barth: Un théologien," 137–47, especially 144–46. See also Lacelle, "Pour une épistémologie," 47–73, especially 64–66.

36. Collins, "Barth's Relationship to Schleiermacher," 213–24, especially 217–21.

37. Barth, *Anselm*, 38–39.

The Feeling of Transcendence, an Experience of God?

experience, either of the Word of God or the "experience of His work and sign."[38] While this is certainly within the wider perspective of a repudiation of mysticism,[39] it is still possible to detect here the seed of an appreciation of the anthropological underpinning which will be critical to his writings in volume IV.

Second, Barth's appreciation of the value of non-biblical and non-ecclesial words of wisdom that can be heard from the cosmos is an indirect acknowledgment of his openness to transcendent experiences, even though he does not specifically study them. He is clearly aware of the danger inherent in such experiences: namely, the possibility that someone with a religious sensibility would enjoy their own infinitude while never truly opening up to the Transcendent. In this respect, Barth offers a serious warning, which would be unwise to dismiss, since it is aligned with the wisdom of the great spiritual masters, whether Christian or not.

Third, Barth does not undertake a systematic analysis of mysticism. Jean-Louis Leuba, an expert in Barthian thought, points out that he must be read as "a preacher, a prophet who offers an essentially kerygmatic message."[40] With this in mind, Leuba offers two important qualifications.

The first takes into account a better understanding of mysticism:

> Barth emphasized that, within the whole as he saw it, a difference and a distance continue to exist: this difference and this distance are not really unknown in mysticism. In the same way, it is possible to completely separate mysticism and faith in the Word, as if there were two opposing forms of religion.[41]

This insightful critique implies that the criteria for discernment that apply to transcendent experiences are not exclusively Christian. Other spiritual traditions have proposed practical

---

38. Barth, *CD*, vol. 7, II/1/1, §25, 57.

39. Barth, *CD*, vol. 7, II/1/1, §25, 55–56.

40. Leuba, *Études barthiennes*, 5–6 (this translation and those following are based on Leuba's French text); see also 136.

41. Leuba, *Études barthiennes*, 127.

A Prophetic Denunciation?

distinctions between true and false religion, or, more precisely, ways of assessing the level of authenticity of religious experience.

Leuba's second qualification relates to the many authors who have assessed Barth's thought on the subject:

> It seems to me impossible not to agree with those who, since the beginning and later, considered that Barth's theological thought, despite his denials, involves a positive recognition of something that we can and must see as mystical, that is the union, in the human person's conscience – that is, in the person *themselves* – of the awareness/knowledge that God has of himself and that the person has of God.[42]

When God shares his own knowledge of himself, the ensuing mystical experience, whether it turns out to be simply undeveloped or cultivated over time, has a real value. In the context of this inquiry, this means that transcendent experiences that happen in non-Christian contexts may well be the work of the Holy Spirit.

In summary, we find in Barth two propositions that are not contradictory, although they are certainly in tension with each other. The first, which is more striking because of the author's insistence upon it, is an oft-repeated warning about the danger of a human-centric withdrawal into transcendent experiences. The second, from his post–Second World War writings, is an invitation to pay attention to non-biblical and non-ecclesial revelations that can be identified in the cosmos and in history. It is legitimate to see these two viewpoints of Barth's as able to be integrated into a Christian vision that recognizes critically the validity of transcendent experiences. In spite of appearances, his theology of the Holy Spirit at work in the cosmos and in history reveals an openness to transcendent experiences.

---

42. Leuba, *Études barthiennes*, 125.

6

Critiques

The middle of the twentieth century gave rise to a fundamental change in approach in the areas of psychology and theology. The shift was from a "nothing but" attitude (as in "religious experience is *nothing but* the result of psychological mechanisms") to an "it depends" attitude aimed at assessing the validity of concrete religious expressions. Generally, psychologists as well as theologians stopped taking positions simply for or against religion and tried to discern, in a more nuanced way, the authentic from the inauthentic.

From Rejection to Critique

Interestingly, this shift was anticipated by Stendhal, one of the great French writers of the nineteenth century, who himself moves from an attitude of rejection to one of discernment. René Girard points this out:

> In the early Stendhal and in some of his essays we find an opposition, inherited from the eighteenth century, between the lucid skepticism of honest people and the hypocritical religion of everyone else. In his great works this opposition has disappeared. It has been replaced by a

Critiques

contrast between the hypocritical religion of the vain and the 'true' religion of the passionate.[1]

Today, few psychologists simply reject the phenomenon of religion out of hand. However, aberrations within religion continue to be the object of study. The solid discoveries that were made in the context of the *rejection* of religion are now the basis of the *critique* of religion. Thus, many of Freud's contributions are appreciated: the importance of infantile sexuality, the originality of psychic affectivity, which at first is unconscious and then bears upon conscious processes, the stages of human development, the Oedipus complex, many psychological mechanisms (censure, repression, projection, etc.), and therapeutic techniques (attentiveness to dreams, free association, etc.).

Furthermore, the psychoanalytical critiques of religion have found their way into the world of theology. As an example, a chapter in *Initiation à la pratique de la théologie* (Initiation to theological practice) addresses the pitfalls of religiosity and the contribution of psychoanalysis in purifying Christian faith.[2] Freud's impassioned concern for the truth in the realm of psychology is thus included in the Greek and Christian tradition of self-awareness.

This change in attitude finds articulate expression in the work of psychoanalyst Eric Fromm. His essay on the dogma of Christ, published in German in 1930 and clearly inspired by Freud's ideas, reveals his suspicion of Christianity, which he explains away solely in terms of psychological mechanisms and socio-political conditioning. The author did not realize that he was cutting off his nose to spite his face. Indeed, if Christian thought could be boiled down to mechanisms and conditioning, on what basis could Fromm claim that his writings about Christianity were nothing other than a reflection of the psycho-socio-political determinism that lies behind and impacted them? In the Foreword that he wrote to the 1963 edition of the essay, Fromm states, with

---

1. Girard, *Deceit*, 65.
2. Lebeaux, "Les critiques psychanalytiques"; see 493–506.

The Feeling of Transcendence, an Experience of God?

admirable honesty, that he clearly disagrees with several of the conclusions presented in his original essay.[3]

In 1950, twenty years after that essay was first published, he espoused another, quite different position, which he presented at the Terry Lectures at Yale University; it was published under the title *Psychoanalysis and Religion*. Here he interprets Freud's *The Future of an Illusion* as a denunciation of *false* religion:

> Freud holds that the aim of human development is the achievement of these ideals: knowledge (reason, truth, *logos*), brotherly love, reduction of suffering, independence, and responsibility. . . . Freud speaks in the name of the ethical core of religion and criticizes the theistic-supernatural concepts of religion for preventing the full realization of these ethical aims. . . . The statement that Freud is 'against' religion therefore is misleading unless we define sharply *what* religion and what aspects of religion he is critical of and what aspects of religion he speaks for.[4]

While taking into account Freud's moral position, Fromm moves from the "nothing but" to the "it depends" approach. In tackling the "problem of religion and psychoanalysis," he writes that he wants "to show that to set up alternatives of either irreconcilable opposition or identity of interest is fallacious . . . ."[5] He uses Freud's ethical criteria to refocus the discussion: "the question is not whether man returns to religion and believes in God but whether he lives love and thinks truth."[6]

In Fromm's view, the era of generalizations about religion is over, since "no intelligent discussion of the problem is possible as long as we deal with religion in general instead of differentiating between various types of religion and religious experience." A little further on, he states that within the various types of religion, the most important distinction is "that between *authoritarian* and

---

3. Fromm, *Dogma of Christ*, vii–x and 1–91.
4. Fromm, *Psychoanalysis and Religion*, 18–19.
5. Fromm, *Psychoanalysis and Religion*, 9.
6. Fromm, *Psychoanalysis and Religion*, 9.

humanistic religions."[7] This distinction provides the assessment principles for religious attitudes that can be observed.

On the one hand, authoritarian religion relies on an infantile obedience to the almighty authority of God, on a loss of independence and integrity as an individual, on a denial of a person's value and strength. In Fromm's view, this is Calvin's religion.[8] Humanistic religion, meanwhile, involves developing a person's reason and capacity for love to foster understanding, experience solidarity with all living beings, move to self-realization, and feel joy rather than distress and guilt. For Fromm, it is the religion of early Buddhism, of Taoism, of Isaiah, of Jesus, and of Socrates.[9]

Finally, in his 1956 book, *The Art of Loving*, he roots religion in the need to overcome separateness and in the desire for wholeness. He dismisses the aberration or inadequacy of certain means of escaping isolation (orgiastic states, conformism, even creative activity) and sees love as the only solution. In love, he differentiates between symbiotic union and mature love. Symbiotic union can be passive (submission, masochism) or active (domination, sadism). Mature love is, in contrast, a union or a participation that comes about through inner freedom, preserving personal integrity.[10]

This union-participation that preserves personal integrity will serve as the touchstone, to which we will return, to assess the authenticity of religious experience. This passage from *Psychoanalysis and Religion* is representative of this healthy attitude, which Fromm calls "oneness with the world":

> It is an attitude of oneness not only in oneself, not only with one's fellow men, but with all life and, beyond that, with the universe. Some may think that this attitude is one in which the uniqueness and individuality of the self are denied and the experience of self weakened. That this is not so constitutes the paradoxical nature of this attitude. It comprises both the sharp and even painful

---

7. Fromm, *Psychoanalysis and Religion*, 34.
8. Fromm, *Psychoanalysis and Religion*, 34–37.
9. Fromm, *Psychoanalysis and Religion*, 37–38; on love, see also 86–87.
10. Fromm, *Art of Loving*, 7–21.

The Feeling of Transcendence, an Experience of God?

awareness of one's self as a separate and unique entity and the longing to break through the confines of this individual organization and to be one with the All. The religious attitude in this sense is simultaneously the fullest experience of individuality and of its opposite; it is not so much a blending of the two as a polarity from whose tension religious experience springs. It is an attitude of pride and integrity and at the same time of a humility which stems from experiencing oneself as but a thread in the texture of the universe.[11]

The Oceanic Feeling

For Freud, as we have seen, religion represents an irreversible regression to an infantile state. Many psychologists have broadened and nuanced these Freudian ideas, and have acknowledged that in art and in human love, as well as in religion, a person is subject to a temporary regression in service of the ego.[12] Rollo May, in his book on creativity, sees the use of this concept of regression in the case of intellectual and artistic creativity as being inadequate and unsatisfactory. He suggests a more balanced view as he points out that symbol and myth have both a regressive side and a progressive side. The artist regresses inasmuch as he or she allows fears and archaic desires to surface, but progresses when this primitive psychic material serves to bring meaning and form to a reality that lies before him or her. Their awareness of this reality is so intense that only the term "ecstasy" does it justice.[13] As in the creative act, the accounts of transcendence that we examined at the beginning of this book carry within them a call to move forward, which can powerfully reorient a person to the future.

11. Fromm, *Psychoanalysis and Religion*, 95.

12. See, for example, Kris, *Psychoanalytic Explorations in Art*, 59, 167, 291–302; Maslow, *Psychology of Being*, 105–6. Note, however, the critique of some of Maslow's ideas in Vergote, *Religious Man*, 155–56. Still, Vergote also recognizes the idea of a healthy regression short of a dissociation between the reality principle and the pleasure principle.

13. May, *Courage to Create*, 88–94.

Critiques

May's reflections have a bearing on the oceanic feeling, this transcendent experience—of the aesthetic type—which I briefly alluded to as I discussed Freud's *Civilization and Its Discontents*. In the first part of that book,[14] he sets the stage by stating that one day he received a letter from a prominent man (we know that man to be Romain Rolland). In the letter, the writer suggests that the true source of religiosity consists in a particular feeling that never leaves him, and that has been confirmed by many other people. He calls it a "sensation of 'eternity', a feeling as of something limitless, unbounded—as it were, 'oceanic' . . . , a feeling of an indissoluble bond, of being one with the external world as a whole."[15]

Freud keenly detects in this phenomenon the connection of an intellectual preconception and an affective element rather than an immediate and pure feeling that would shed light on the ties that bind the human being and the surrounding world. This observation is in line with the views expressed in the first few chapters of this book on the ideas and questions that set the stage for the emergence of the feeling of transcendence.

Freud then reminds the reader that the boundaries of the ego are not always stationary. In the state of being in love, for example, the boundary between the ego and the other tends to dissolve. At this point, however, Freud unfortunately locks himself into a particular view: such a phenomenon can only be explained by either a physiological function or a pathological process. As already mentioned, he makes no allowance here for an intentionality that would be linked to the physiological function.[16]

In his view, as the boundaries of the ego become blurred and the ego feels one with the universe, the ego relives an all-encompassing infantile feeling. However, I very much doubt that it is possible for the toddler to feel an openness to a vast expanse. It appears that while being rooted in this undifferentiated infantile condition,

---

14. Freud, "Civilization," 63–74.
15. Freud, "Civilization," 64–65.
16. See Roy, *Coherent Christianity*, chapter 3, section entitled "Openness to Reality."

The Feeling of Transcendence, an Experience of God?

a sense of the infinite must somehow be acquired through a certain sensory, imaginative, and cognitive development.

That point is made by Walter Houston Clark in an article in which he draws on Henry Elkin's work.[17] Both acknowledge that a primordial state—one that is both undifferentiated and of total happiness—recurs in an adult's mystical experience. While this original state forms the prototype of the mystical experience, there is a considerable difference. People who are faced with certain features of a state experienced during early childhood nevertheless carry within them all that they have acquired during the long period of development that follows childhood. These resources allow the individual to open up to a world that seems limitless, becoming one with it in a way that does not eliminate all differentiation, even though it is a psychic union modeled on a childhood memory.

Freud is therefore correct when he sees recollections of early childhood in the oceanic feeling. He is unfortunately incorrect when he comes to the conclusion that such a feeling is irrevocably infantile in nature. Besides, as he freely admits, he has never had a feeling like the one Romain Rolland describes. It is significant that Freud did no research on this subject,[18] that he never wrote about Eastern religions, and that he concedes that he was mostly concerned with common forms of religiosity—rather mediocre in Austria in his time—that he witnessed in the lives of his contemporaries.[19]

His stoic resignation and his preference for scientific work result in a failure to draw upon the richest and deepest sources of religious feeling. In this, he is not alone. Karlfried Graf von Dürckheim tells the story of a conversation he once had as a psychotherapist. The man he was talking to was well off, in good health, and had no family troubles, but complained of unexplainable feelings of anxiety, guilt, and emptiness. In Dürckheim's view, the man's great dissatisfaction was due to his denial of "his essential Being."

---

17. Clark, "Mysticism," 47–58, especially 53–54. See also Elkin, "Origin of the Self," 57–76.
18. Bamberger, "Religion as Illusion?" 42.
19. Zilboorg, *Psychoanalysis and Religion*, 221.

Critiques

Such a denial goes hand in hand with a life philosophy that extols efficiency: "Achievement is all."[20]

Meanwhile, Abraham H. Maslow, in a book on peak-experiences,[21] examines people who seem incapable of having transcendent experiences. In fact, these "non-peakers" have often had at least one such experience, but they have either been unable to identify it as such or have dismissed it as unimportant. Of the people who believe they have to defend themselves from transcendent experiences, he includes those whose philosophical outlook is rationalistic, materialistic, mechanistic, or logical-positivist; those who can only control their behavior through denial or unrelenting control of their emotions; those who are so pragmatic that they pour all their energy into finding ways to achieve concrete results; and those who are so extroverted that they pay no attention to what is going on within themselves.

Maslow, who has an excessive tendency to generalize, points out that "non-peakers" are found among the clergy and religious leaders. In a reference to the legend of the Grand Inquisitor from Dostoevsky's *The Brothers Karamazov*, he refers to the paradox arising from the fact that in churches and sects, "non-peakers" are often given the official responsibility to convey a religious experience of which they have no knowledge! When he considers ways in which a memory could be roused in those who in reality are more "weak peakers" than "non-peakers," he states that proper therapy should include eliminating inhibitions, blockages, and fears with regard to the transcendent experience, as well as paying close attention to its presence in a person's lived experience.

The Mother's or Father's Religion?

Freud refuses to consider the oceanic feeling as the main source of religion. In his view, the sole source of religion is a much more powerful need: that of paternal protection. Unlike the oceanic

---

20. von Dürckheim, *Two-fold Origin*, 21–22.
21. Maslow, *Religions*, 19–29 and 84–90.

The Feeling of Transcendence, an Experience of God?

feeling, which is but the reinstatement of the infant's unlimited narcissism, the need for a father endures through human anxiety in the face of destiny. Freud concedes, however, that the feeling of being one with the Universe is also a search for religious solace, a way to deny any and all danger coming from the outside world.

Given the similarities between the mother and nature, the oceanic feeling relates to an environment seen as being clearly maternal. Melanie Klein and Joan Riviere's observation supports this assertion: "The relation to nature which arouses such strong feelings of love, appreciation, admiration and devotion, has much in common with the relation to one's mother, as has long been recognized by poets."[22]

There is a need to rebalance the relationship between these two forms of religiosity—one centered on the father and the other centered on the mother—since each of them reflects a particular way for the psyche to shape the transcendent experience. This is the approach suggested by psychoanalyst Jean-Claude Sagne in an article where he shows the complementary nature of the maternal and paternal aspects of religious experience.[23]

Drawing on the theories of Klein and Riviere, he first examines the maternal relationship. It is an ambivalent one. On the one hand, the mother represents the instant and sufficient satisfying of needs—in a word, happiness—by the fact that she provides sustenance and warmth, rest and safety, affection and essential care. On the other hand, the nursing breast, which the infant wants to suckle and empty, represents a threat of destruction. This is the result of protection and identification mechanisms that characterize the relationship at an oral level, in which the infant fears the loss of its individuality by being reabsorbed into the maternal womb. A mother is therefore at the same time a figure of bliss and a figure of death. For the human being, joy can seemingly be attained only by the loss of their personal life.

Turning to the paternal relationship, Sagne holds to the universality of the Oedipus complex, amid cultural variations, which

---

22. Klein and Riviere, *Love, Hate and Reparation*, 107–8.
23. Sagne, "De l'illusion," 38–58, especially 46–58.

Critiques

in his view do not challenge the basic structure.[24] Of this complex, what affects the relation to God is all that is of interest here. While feeling guilty for wanting to kill the father, the child also receives the Law from the father—a major theme in Jacques Lacan's work. The child can either see this Law as an arbitrary diktat or as the enactment of something necessary that forms part of reality. If the child accepts such a necessity, he understands his fundamental lack and accepts the father as a model with which the child can identify. From that moment, he understands that the mediation of others and delayed gratification are necessary conditions to be met on the road to becoming fully human.

Sagne rightly insists on the importance of giving up the all-powerful illusion of one's desire by accepting that such desire must be mediated through human interactions. It is when a person becomes deeply aware that their existence originates from an Other, over which they have no control, that they can accept their finiteness. At that point a person moves from the imaginary to the symbolic, although the imaginary will always remain an anthropological substratum. Indeed, the imaginary is controlled by the projection and anxiety about the father, while the symbolic establishes the mysterious presence of a Father beyond any subjective representations. The maturing of this relationship to God requires a work of mourning, as Freud would say, toward an infantile way of satisfying one's desires—a never-ending task.

In a study entitled "The Two Axes of Religion,"[25] Antoine Vergote presents thoughts similar to Sagne's. He sets the oceanic feeling in close relationship to the mother figure. He believes that the mother image that is imprinted in the human psyche can either impede the healthy development of a personality or be an affective conduit with rich possibilities. The ancient memory of the primordial whole and life-giving renewal can either imprison a person in the past or direct them toward the future in an active

---

24. Based on Ortigues and Ortigues, *Oedipe africain*, who discuss the objections raised by Malinowski.

25. Published in Vergote, *Religious Man*, 143–200. See also Vergote, *Guilt and Desire*, 121–35.

The Feeling of Transcendence, an Experience of God?

and mature search for a better world. The oceanic feeling, evoking universal harmony, does not necessarily lead us back to a paradise lost, but it could spur people to build a new city. There is, however, a condition: the relationship with the father, who gives a Law that is both limitation and promise, places believers within a symbolic network marked by realism.

A comparison of two authors will conclude our illustration of the relationships between the oceanic feeling, marked by the relation to the mother, and the adult acceptance of human finiteness. Yves Lebeaux, who was mentioned earlier,[26] embraces a totally negative approach regarding the "archaic Mother." He states that the totally satisfying union with such a Mother is a phantasmic desire and thus is fundamentally illusory. In his view, this desire is even deadly, since it goes against the process of individuation and separation that constitutes human personhood. Against a religion of dependency, where a person projects their fantasies onto God, he sets human autonomy, where one learns to desire for oneself.

Lebeaux's views are clearly a step backward compared to the more balanced positions of Sagne and Vergote. Sebastian Moore offers a much richer treatment than Lebeaux of the same subject.[27] Drawing on the work of psychoanalyst Margaret Mahler, whom I will discuss in the next chapter, Moore sees in childhood two poles of attraction: the oceanic lure of the maternal breast and the awareness of being separated from it. People live their whole lives in the tension between these two poles. When this tension is not reduced to a simple compromise between dreamed bliss and the harsh reality of a finite existence, it can be perfectly healthy.

In fact, at each turning point or crisis in life, the ego—under the combined influence of a concrete event and the oceanic vector—reconstitutes itself. A person leaves behind a way of functioning that had worked until then, to acquire a hitherto unknown way of being and acting in the world. A new subject emerges, richer

---

26. Lebeaux, "Les critiques psychanalytiques," 493–507, especially 498, 499, and 502.

27. For a presentation of Moore's thought, see Roy, *Coherent Christianity*, chapter 6.

than before, through suffering and enlightenment, in the experience of a series of deaths of transitional forms of the ego. In this way, the tension between union and separation is fruitful, since it enables rebirth and growth as a human being. The vectors of union and separation do not, as might be supposed, operate independently of one another. Moore brings them together by drawing on a psychology of desire that is quite different from those of Freud and Lebeaux. For those two thinkers, a stoic mistrust sees desire as infantile and craving an illusory infinite; in Moore's thought, on the other hand, intentionality, while remaining realistic, is open to the infinite.

In this chapter, I wanted to show the fundamental change of attitude in the world of the psychology of religion over the last fifty years or so. The shift was generally from a Freudian "nothing but" to "it depends," because of the recognition that religious experience actually has both positive and negative effects. Also, rather than speaking of the so-called illusory nature of religion, a neutral approach to religion's cognitive and moral validity was adopted. This change in methodology opens the door to the approach proposed in the next chapter, where we will use assessment criteria from psychology, philosophy, and traditional mystical wisdom.

7

Validation

In this chapter, I will touch upon some of the fundamental issues related to the validity of transcendent experiences. The discussion will cover the following topics: the relationship between intentionality and the Holy Spirit; the psyche and the road to maturity; the relative importance of self-awareness and otherness; the question of evil and the non-experience of God; and the role of spiritual guides.

Intentionality and the Holy Spirit

Through our analysis of Feuerbach's, Freud's, and Fromm's thought in the preceding chapters, I pointed out the unsustainable position that transcendent experiences are only the psychological projection of a person's subjective desires. If that were the case, it would be impossible to defend not only a certain religious objectivity, but also a scientific and philosophical objectivity. We compared the image of cutting off one's nose to spite one's face to this contradiction.

In chapter 4, I mentioned the importance of human intentionality, the spontaneous movement of openness to the world. Intentionality is "tension toward." It tends to take in reality in all its forms, such as sensible, meaningful, valuable, and personal.

Validation

Thanks to intentionality, what is true in the theories of Feuerbach or Freud cannot be reduced to the projection of their desires.

Furthermore, because of intentionality, transcendent experiences are far from being illusions: they open us up to the Infinite. But while these experiences *are a window* to the Infinite, they do not *provide* the Infinite: it is the not-finite, rather than the Infinite, that occurs phenomenologically. When human intentionality senses something that is totally beyond it, it feels that it is being moved toward a cosmic whole, a global meaning, an immeasurable value, or an unconditional love. Yet all that can be said from a philosophical perspective is that what is seen, as it were, is a reflection of the Infinite in the human soul; what is heard, as it were, is a single echo within intentional dynamism. Although they involve, through the attraction they offer, momentum toward God, transcendent experiences remain unable, in and of themselves, to reach God. From this emerges the apophatic view that speaks of their end in terms of "neither this, nor that," since their end always remains beyond our ideas or feelings.

Catholic theology, drawing on the writings of St. Paul and St. John, teaches that there is no true contact with God unless he freely chooses to be present and to be experienced, through grace. The notion of being freely given is present in all three great monotheistic religions, but also in the works of the Greek philosopher Plotinus and in numerous Hindu texts as well. We saw this in chapter 2, in a passage from the Bhagavad Gita where Krishna says to Arjuna: "A celestial eye I'll give you." The unreachable God allows himself to be reached. This does not do away with the negative aspect, but balances it with a positive one: namely, an extraordinary gift. This explains why, whether right away or at a later time, a transcendent experience can be understood as God's presence. The feeling that the whole of creation turns out to be inadequate and the feeling of completeness that pervades our consciousness are sufficient grounds to reasonably affirm that the Holy Spirit has touched us, both in our feelings and in our thoughts. The feeling of transcendence is often an experience of God.

The Feeling of Transcendence, an Experience of God?

The Psyche and the Road to Maturity

As they move from the view that religion is "nothing but" to saying "it depends," most psychologists today now offer more nuanced reflections, which take into account various criteria of discernment. As an example, it is perfectly legitimate to wonder whether alternating between periods of transcendent experiences and times of emotional disinterest might be a sign of bipolar disorder. An "it depends" inquiry will answer the question by saying that this is certainly the case for some people, but not for others.

In the case of a person who does not have bipolar disorder, the alternation simply stems from the fact that he or she cannot sustain for extended periods a highly emotional openness to the infinite. A healthier person will naturally move from religious feeling to peaceful belief in a Presence who remains even when the feeling has passed. The end of the experience is not understood as a dramatic loss, nor does it lead to an unhealthy nostalgia.

However, persons with bipolar disorder will find it difficult to live with the alternation. During the peak-experience, their emotional state is heightened, followed by depression. This still does not discount their religious experience. It all depends on how people with the disorder react to their difficulty. If they recognize both the value of their peak-experience and the usefulness of the period of indifference that follows, they will work to develop a certain equanimity. This necessarily difficult learning process will lead the person through considerable psycho-spiritual growth. Such a situation reveals the possibility of collaboration between the psyche and intentionality.

Faulty psychological functioning does not negate a human being's openness to the infinite. What psychologists conclude in such cases is that there is a lack of fruitfulness. When the psyche is askew, transcendent experiences do not produce the same remarkable results that we observe in people with stronger egos. However, these experiences are not totally unfruitful: people can encounter God and maintain a basic hope while knowing they are psychically and morally miserable. It is possible to grow in faith, hope, and

Validation

love while making no progress on the psychic level. It goes without saying that the ideal is growth in all aspects of life. In most cases, the fruits of a religious experience extend to other areas of life, but at times, such an experience results in holding onto a minimum level of hope, without noticing any other concrete results.

In many cases of inauthentic religious experience, it seems that a person's intentionality, as well as his or her psyche, are not well oriented. Some members of sects or churches, for example, have abused their power, committed financial fraud, or sexually exploited others. In such cases, it is the ethical side of intentionality that is lacking. Psychiatrist Karlfried Graf von Dürckheim, who was presented briefly in chapter 1, wisely insists on the importance of balancing the "inner person" and the "outer person," of rounding out religious initiation with moral education or psychotherapy.[1]

It can happen that people who are not fully functional psychologically or morally can still make use of some of the potential found in a transcendent experience. In this way, they can adjust how they use their intentionality in everyday life. This striking event in their lives does not lead to a sense of nostalgia, but triggers a forward momentum. The memory of their experience will help them to enhance their present situation. Their basic attitude is not oriented toward the past but, on the contrary, is a creative outlook toward the future.

Chapter 1 of the book *Critical Incidents in Psychotherapy* is entitled "Don't Give Me Up!" It presents the case of Tom, a young criminal who, after a certain amount of time in a clinical relationship, makes this plea to his psychologist: "If you give me up, then there is no hope for me."[2] Far from letting him down, the psychologist gives Tom ten one-on-one counseling sessions, one hour per week—the amount permitted by the detention center. Then he loses sight of Tom. Four months later, Tom contacts the psychologist to relate a transcendent experience that had taken him by surprise:

---

1. See Roy, *Coherent Christianity*, 137–38; also see 106–9.
2. Standal and Corsini, *Critical Incidents*, 3.

The Feeling of Transcendence, an Experience of God?

> The funniest thing happened to me Saturday. I don't know if I am crazy or what. Nothing like this ever happened before. I was walking across the big yard, going over to a group of people I knew, and as I was walking I suddenly experienced something. It came over me like a cloud. I couldn't move. Suddenly I felt peaceful and happy. I felt clean, pure, good, and wonderful. I never experienced such a feeling of happiness. I don't know how long it lasted. Maybe a second, maybe a minute. I have only a memory of it, but I do know that this feeling had something to do with you.[3]

The explanation given by a number of psychiatrists and psychologists who review the case in the book is that the relation between the therapist and Tom, in which he felt welcomed and hopeful, played the role of intermediary that made Tom's experience of emotional wholeness possible. After sharing it with the therapist and indirectly expressing his gratitude for the therapist's role in it, Tom was eventually released from prison and actively reintegrated into society. There he found a steady job, bought a house, got married, and raised a child. In short, his intentionality successfully adjusted to life's demands. In his remarks about the case, Viktor Frankl observes that it all started with the return to a religious connection (*religio* in the sense of relationship), a contact that until then had been repressed but that suddenly resurfaced during a highly meaningful event.[4] The validity of the religious event can be measured by its fruitfulness in everyday life.

Self-awareness and Otherness

We have just seen that the validity of the religious experience depends on psychic conditions as well as intentionality. Taking things a step further reveals that authentic intentionality naturally emphasizes otherness. In turn, otherness includes paying attention

---

3. Standal and Corsini, *Critical Incidents*, 4.
4. See the case description and discussion, 1–17.

Validation

to the other and to God.⁵ In the previous section of this chapter, I focused on intentionality from a *moral* perspective—the respect due to others. In this section, I wish to examine intentionality from a *religious* perspective—a person's openness to God.

In chapter 2, which presented purely phenomenological considerations, I spoke of the transcendent experience as an awareness of our openness to the not-finite. I did not discuss the issue of the ontological status of this in-finite there. My comparison with the aesthetic experience revealed that human intentionality is spontaneously aimed at real "objects." These objects are not simply things perceived by the senses, but also aesthetic, cultural, and spiritual. I think that a convincing philosophical argument can make the case for the existence of the Infinite in and of itself: that it is not a limited "object" and that it is distinct from any and all finite beings. I cannot go down that rather long road in this book, as it would involve many nuances and too much time.

In this section, I will limit myself to the following argument: for the person who has had a transcendent experience, it is instructive to interpret the event not only as simply reaching a state that goes beyond day-to-day awareness, but as an encounter with the Other, who is both fascinating and formidable. Of course, a feeling of transcendence is not, in and of itself, an experience *of God*. However, within Catholic theology, it is possible to affirm that divine grace can use this feeling to bring about such an experience, the place of a true encounter with the Infinite.⁶

It is also important to extend this brief encounter and make of it a sustained presence to an incomparable Presence. In other words, it would be a serious mistake to simply stop at the level of self-awareness, even if this self is the best a person can be. Only being focused on the Other will completely satisfy the deep desire, which is to communicate, to be known and to know, to be loved and to love.

In the previous chapter, I presented the model of a paternal-maternal God or, to put it within a biblical framework, a God who

---

5. Roy, *Coherent Christianity*, chapter 9.
6. See Lonergan, *Method in Theology*, chapter 4.

The Feeling of Transcendence, an Experience of God?

is a father with several maternal traits.[7] Our relationship to the Infinite is psychically shaped by our initial relationship with our father or mother, or with the people who filled this role for us. As a general rule (even though there are exceptions), the father is more likely to represent a distancing, while the mother is more likely to represent closeness in relation to the child. Mahler and colleagues suggest that from the fourth or fifth month to the thirtieth or thirty-sixth month, the infant grows into a young child, moving from a stage of absorption in the mother to a stage of separation-individuation.[8]

While Mahler and colleagues do not apply their psychoanalytical discoveries to the relationship with God, we find in their book the valuable idea of an equilibrium between belonging and differentiation that is also found in Fromm, Dürckheim, and Moore. Two extremes are to be avoided: fusion with the impersonal and depersonalizing Universe, and individualistic isolation. To be fruitful, the union felt during a transcendent experience must foster an attitude that excludes both fusion and isolation. The relationship between the human being and God is therefore a union in differentiation. On the one hand, there will be a powerful desire for union, sometimes followed by a sense of complete union with the Source, beyond images or concepts.[9] On the other hand, there will be differentiation between the human person in regard to the Other who captivates them.

How do we measure this? I would suggest two ways. The first is religious, in that the differentiation will be revealed as a renunciation of a false sense of peace related to an infantile symbiosis.

---

7. See Roy, "Inclusive Language," 207–15.

8. See Mahler et al., *Psychological Birth*, 3–8 for an overview. Their analysis revolves around the mother/child relationship. Regarding the father, they note on page 91: "Although he is not fully outside the symbiotic union, neither is he ever fully part of it."

9. As the Song of Songs strongly suggests, mystical union is modeled on erotic union. About the latter, Freud notes: "At the height of being in love the boundary between ego and object threatens to melt away. Against all the evidence of his senses, a man who is in love declares that 'I' and 'you' are one . . . ." Freud, "Civilization," 66.

Validation

In this way, the relation to God is characterized by a conforming of human desire to the will of the Other, with full acceptance of the consequences. The second way to measure is moral. It consists of recognizing reality and its demands—Mahler and colleagues speak of "reality testing."[10] This reality is first and foremost all the people to whom one must adjust. Openness to the Other is thus demonstrated by an openness to others.

The ability to find a balance between union and differentiation in the relationship with God greatly depends on how this balance was lived out between the child and the parents. Surrendering to the Infinite and taking adult responsibility in a finite world are based on reactions that began to form in early childhood. But for many people, surrendering to God seems rather dangerous! There is a fear of getting hurt, or of "reengulfment."[11] For others, it seems dangerous to make decisions that are not dictated by God or by parents! The weak ego cannot break away from the things that infantilize it. It is easy to stay within one of these two extremes: moral control that is closed to Mystery, or religious feeling accompanied by human immaturity.

Looking back to the four families of mindsets of transcendent experiences described in chapter 3, we realize that transcendent experiences contain unequal possibilities in regard to an openness to the Other. Thus, even though the aesthetic type, with its cosmic orientation, is probably the most common, it often produces only a simple harmony within a larger whole, a pantheistic fusion, an oceanic feeling, delight in having reached a higher consciousness—all of this without moral transformation. The ontological type provides a glimpse of a Being who is completely different from all other beings, but the meaning found there often remains impersonal. There is a trust in destiny that remains agnostic or skeptical toward the Author of this destiny. The ethical type has the advantage of offering an invitation to commit to values, but these are easily distorted and become idols.

---

10. Mahler et al., *Psychological Birth*, 6.
11. Mahler et al., *Psychological Birth*, 10.

The Feeling of Transcendence, an Experience of God?

It is most often during the interpersonal type of transcendent experience that the sense of unlimited love is clearly perceived as a gift from a Reality who is not "infrapersonal" but rather very personal or, to be more precise, "suprapersonal."[12] Whether we call this Reality "God" or some other name, it is revealed and enters into dialogue with the human being, who then knows that he or she is called to an unconditional openness. What is more, the perspective gained due to the interpersonal type enriches the meaning brought to the other three types. In this way, the aesthetic, the ontological, and the ethical types can be seen as interpersonal meeting places.

Furthermore, in the context of non-theistic meditation, the personal nature of God is problematic because it is seen as limiting. The difficulty lies in the notion that personalist language could express a suprapersonal Reality. The nuanced solution to this quandary proposed by thinkers such as Augustine and Thomas Aquinas is not widely known.[13] Nevertheless, such an intellectual hurdle does not prevent many meditators from forgetting themselves and centering themselves on an unnamable Reality. A healthy human intentionality focuses on a value other than itself in which it recognizes, even if only intuitively, transcendent nature. In other words, an extended contemplative practice can result in self-transcendence, without any reference to a personal God.

That being said, the fact remains that an explicit attentiveness to the otherness of the divine enables a person to be freed more quickly from the lure of the experience itself. We can, in fact, show more interest in our experience, with the feelings, states of consciousness, and discoveries it involves, than in the Reality to which the experience should lead us. Many close themselves off to this Reality, victims of the widespread belief that religious experience is first and foremost a matter of personal fulfillment.

---

12. See the thoughtful remarks and the quotations from texts of the three monotheistic religions in Barzel, *Mystique de l'Ineffable*, 42–48, to be supplemented with 135–42.

13. This solution is presented in Roy, *Coherent Christianity*, 145–49. See also Pelletier, *Les Dieux*, 69–71.

Validation

Any gains remain at the level of the ego, which remains at the center of everything, even though a divine gift may have been acknowledged.

These considerations explain why this book does not delve into the so-called mystical effects of drugs. In some cases, drug use brings about something akin to a transcendent experience. But let us recall that the transcendent experience has been defined not as a mystical state, but as a simple openness to the infinite. It seems that drugs can at times trigger such an openness, but they will rarely bear the tangible fruits of a lasting religious discovery, a stable mystical state of consciousness, or positive moral consequences.[14] The whole process is rendered nearly invalid by the fact that it starts with a desire for a drug-induced experience. The person remains a prisoner of purely subjective feelings, which do nothing to bring about true otherness.

Evil and the Non-experience of God

In a review of *The Living Stream* by Sir Alister Hardy (the zoologist-philosopher introduced in chapter 1), Arthur Koestler wrote: "[t]he most obvious criticism to be levelled against this book by believers and unbelievers alike is that, except for a few passing mentions, it evades the crucial question of evil."[15] It is notable that Koestler, who had had transcendent experiences, is critical of a book about these very phenomena. To his credit, he remains unimpressed by authors who extol the benefits of the parapsychological with a facile optimism.

Some people who develop their sense of transcendence opt for an inner harmony without addressing conflicts of the spiritual life. The divine is thus seen as an extension of a mysterious world, as being integral with finite beings. The divine is reached and valued together with pleasant impressions and feelings. This bias can foster in some people a flight from their profound humanity

---

14. See Kellenberger, "Mysticism and Drugs," 175–91.
15. Koestler, *Drinkers of Infinity*, 172.

The Feeling of Transcendence, an Experience of God?

as they embrace only its bright side, never entering the shadows. Unlike the biblical Jacob in the book of Genesis (32:25–33), the modern Jacob, who is overly timid, refuses to wrestle with the angel and doesn't risk dislocating a hip.

As Rudolf Otto suggests, the realm of holiness is not only fascinating, but also formidable. The transcendent experience offers a glimpse of something that is both supremely good and exceedingly dangerous. Meditators have no choice: if they want to be truthful, they must own up to their uncertainty before a Creator who has put them in a world where troubles are as abundant as blessings. By opening their eyes to evil, meditators enter the quandary of their own ambivalence, with its attraction and its suspicion, its attachment and its resentment before God.

There is thus a need to embrace both the negative and the positive, as we have seen in the Bhagavad Gita and in the writings of such diverse writers as Kant, Otto, Heidegger, and Maritain. A life devoid of the negative is confined to a superficial security, a naive complacency, an optimism that overlooks the troubled waters of human existence. Conversely, the encounter with evil raises an essential question: Is it desirable and possible to accept the two aspects—negative and positive—of reality and to be reconciled with everything? The answer requires total surrender to this Infinite, in which is seen unfailing goodness and an equally radical detachment before all that is finite.[16]

The interpersonal aspect of this question plays an important role, especially if it includes a relationship with Jesus Christ. The fact that he is both fully human and fully the Eternal Son of the Father means that Jesus shares our suffering in the face of evil and frees us from it. His passion and resurrection represent and make real this sharing and liberation, the unfeigned experience of the negative and the positive. In victoriously taking on evil, Christ offers us his Holy Spirit so that we may, in turn, accept reality in all its aspects and help to transfigure it. There is no dichotomy, in such

---

16. Arnaud Desjardins offers a masterful analysis of the question of evil, detachment, and acceptance of everything. See Roy, "Desjardins Part 1," 16–22, continued in Roy, "Desjardins Part 2," 9–14.

Validation

a commitment, between being present to Mystery and being present to society. Quite the opposite is true, as our active presence in the world is endowed with a special quality by the fact that a Presence beyond compare is at work within our deepest consciousness.

Related to the problem of evil, although different from it, is another major challenge: the phenomenon of the non-experience of God. If the Transcendent fascinates us, he necessarily becomes the One whose absence grieves us the most. In the aftermath of a transcendent experience (or of more than one), followed by the gift of gratifying emotions and thoughts, there are times when we feel empty: an emptiness, in fact, of feelings, ideas, and religious interest. The experience gives way to the non-experience of God. The relation to the Transcendent seems to diminish, even to fade away, while it is actually growing deeper.

The inability to relive the experience can lead to disappointment and indifference toward the spiritual. Some people try to recover this wonderful feeling by returning to the privileged place where it happened or by recreating the circumstances in which the feeling struck them. They try to return to the past rather than reflecting on their relationship with this Reality that has touched them. They keep trying to nurture transcendent experiences for their own sake, not realizing that growth and peace lie ahead, beyond these experiences, in a step that will inevitably be disorienting and upsetting.

The opportunity that is then offered to us is to glimpse God as the Other, one of a kind, different from anything and anyone we know. Here lies an experience of solitude (which, rather than eliminating solidarity with others, strengthens it). The wonderful thing that can happen in this desert is that the ego retreats into the background while heightening its real interest in God, beyond the benefits gained earlier from the sense of God's presence.

The Feeling of Transcendence, an Experience of God?

The Role of Spiritual Guides

Regarding the usefulness of powerful religious experiences, William James notes that they are an opportune time to move from a normal waking consciousness to a mystical one:

> [O]ur normal waking consciousness, rational consciousness as we call it, is but one special type of consciousness, whilst all about it, parted from it by the filmiest of screens, there lie potential forms of consciousness entirely different. We may go through life without suspecting their existence, but apply the requisite stimulus, and at a touch they are there in all their completeness, definite types of mentality which probably somewhere have their field of application and adaptation. No account of the universe in its totality can be final which leaves these other forms of consciousness quite disregarded. How to regard them is the question, — for they are so discontinuous with ordinary consciousness. Yet they may determine attitudes though they cannot furnish formulas, and open a region though they fail to give a map.[17]

The states of consciousness to which James refers break the undue and strict authority of normal consciousness:

> Yet, I repeat once more, the existence of mystical states absolutely overthrows the pretension of non-mystical states to be the sole and ultimate dictators of what we may believe. . . . It must always remain an open question whether mystical states may not possibly be such superior points of view, windows through which the mind looks out upon a more extensive and inclusive world. . . . yet the counting in of that wider world of meanings, and the serious dealing with it, might, in spite of all the perplexity, be indispensable stages in our approach to the final fullness of the truth.[18]

James then summarizes his belief:

---

17. James, *Varieties of Religious Experience*, 300–301.
18. James, *Varieties of Religious Experience*, 331.

Validation

If, then, there be a wider world of being than that of our every-day consciousness, if in it there be forces whose effects on us are intermittent, if one facilitating condition of the effects be the openness of the "subliminal" door.[19]

I have presented these fairly long quotations from James's work because it is interesting to see this psychologist highlight the importance of moving from normal consciousness to a different order of consciousness, which, when it is cultivated, becomes characteristic of mystical life. Yet the transcendent experience provides an opportunity to discover the difference between consciousness as commonly understood and mystical consciousness. But when human affectivity, touched by the divine, resonates as never before, many recipients of this new gift retreat. They do not think they need to take seriously what has happened to them. They wonder whether their feelings are playing tricks on them and if they are regressing, even to the point of psychosis.

In one of psychiatrist Karlfried Graf von Dürckheim's previously mentioned works, he states the importance of reassuring ordinary people who have had transcendent experiences. He speaks of a woman who, after telling him about such an episode in her life, asks him: "Do you think I ought to take it seriously?" "Yes," he said, "I do mean that, very seriously in fact."[20] Dürckheim refers to this encounter in another book:

> We must first become conscious, be open to the call of Being. At the beginning of spiritual development is the awareness of something entirely different within ourselves. The true spiritual guide is the one who will help us acquire this conscious realization by taking seriously certain experiences that we have had in the course of our lifetime.[21]

The role of the spiritual guide is therefore to encourage people to identify, describe, and interpret their experiences—then,

---

19. James, *Varieties of Religious Experience*, 404.
20. von Dürckheim, *Two-fold Origin*, 48. See 48–50.
21. Goettman, *Dialogue*, 58–59.

The Feeling of Transcendence, an Experience of God?

thanks to this breakthrough, to support their progress toward the Transcendent who is calling them.[22] A person will be able to identify, describe, and interpret his or her experience if the one guiding them has a flexible enough interpretive framework, such as the one presented in this book. In particular, the knowledge of a solid mystical tradition is indispensable to detect the pitfalls that both beginners and those who are more advanced will encounter on their journey.

In the face of the danger that fear will want to censor religious consciousness, the guru will help people develop the organ that will enable them to take transcendence into account. In developing this organ, people fine-tune their spiritual sensibility and strengthen their ability to not abandon the great religious adventure. Spiritual masters will ensure that people who seek them out for support strengthen their relationship to Mystery in growing psychically, morally, and intellectually. These masters will also help people to deal with the challenge of otherness and the absence of God.

---

22. See Roy, *Coherent Christianity*, chapter 8.

8

The Transcendent Experience and Jesus Christ

In post-industrial societies, for at least forty years, we have been witnessing an interiority and mysticism craze. At a time when religious, moral, and social values are being either distorted or radically called into question, many people are searching for spiritual grounding. Their interest is piqued by some of the unique stories presented in the Bible and the writings of other major religions that are mentioned in literary or musical works, reported in sociological studies, or discussed by psychologists, philosophers, and theologians. In this book I have used the term *transcendent experiences* to describe those brief moments during which an individual or group has a sense of being in touch with a dimension or a reality that is completely beyond them. We identified six elements as constituting such experiences: preparation, occasion, feeling, discovery, interpretation, and fruit. We identified four main types: aesthetic, ontological, ethical, and interpersonal.[1]

We know that at the beginning of the nineteenth century, Schleiermacher considered transcendent experience, which he called simply "experience" (as in "inner experience"), as the very

1. For other examples and analyses, see Roy, *Transcendent Experiences*, chapters 1 and 2.

The Feeling of Transcendence, an Experience of God?

center of Christian faith.² Schleiermacher and I disagree somewhat on this point, since the transcendent experience is not the only factor of conversion or openness to God. It does, however, include a potential for conversion and for religious dynamism that is important to take into account in pastoral terms.³

In this chapter, we will explore the transcendent experience as openness to an impersonal divinity, while attempting to show the ways in which it can lead an individual or group to recognize in that experience the presence of a personal God, rather than an impersonal divinity.

Is There a Correct Interpretation?

Among the above-mentioned elements, the fifth one—interpretation—raises a major difficulty: Is it possible to correctly interpret a transcendent experience? In a world marked by relativism, where each and every person allows themselves the right to give personal meaning to life's events, we also find, fortunately, respect for those whose opinions are at odds with our own—a noble attitude that was identified as essential by the Second Vatican Council. Unfortunately, this respect is more often than not expressed in a subjectivist context, which excludes any and all demands for objectivity. Furthermore, this respect entails a disparagement of religious doctrines, which are characterized as "dogmatic." As a result, it is not uncommon for Christians today to receive the skeptical and mocking response that St. Paul had from the Athenians at the Areopagus: "We will hear you again [at another time] about this" (Acts 17:32).

That, in a nutshell, is the difficulty. While clearly noting it, in this chapter I will attempt to sketch an outline of a Christian interpretation of the transcendent experience that many Jews and Muslims—although not all—would agree with. Given that sociological inquiries have shown that such experiences are widespread,

---

2. Regarding Schleiermacher's "experience," see Roy, *Transcendent Experiences*, chapter 4.

3. Roy, "Expériences de transcendance," 459–69.

The Transcendent Experience and Jesus Christ

it is worth heeding them and suggesting a theistic interpretation, one that considers them as an openness to a *personal* God. In this way, some people will see this interpretation as credible, since it will have been related to this aspect of human existence that is the transcendent experience.[4]

An Interpretive Approach

In most cases, the transcendent experience is framed in pantheistic terms, such as contact with an impersonal divinity that is fairly pervasive throughout the cosmos. I disagree with such an explanation, while noting that the experience itself can be authentic and valid without the proposed explanation necessarily being philosophically sustainable. I therefore propose an interpretation in terms of openness to a personal God, even a trinitarian God, who is triply personal. We will do this in light of the four previously identified types of transcendent experience: aesthetic, ontological, ethical, and interpersonal.

The *aesthetic* type of transcendent experience involves pleasure or displeasure toward nature and the cosmos. It comes with an admiration for the multifaceted beauty of our world or, on the contrary, fear or awe before its threat of destruction. It seems to me that this experience could bring about an appreciation for divine Providence, which is mysteriously at work in the universe. It could also be related to a desire to clean up our planet, and thus be an added motivator in the ecological struggle. The image of Christ Pantocrator (Almighty), so important in Byzantine art, might have meaning as the one who guides and leads humanity and the cosmos toward their fulfillment.

The *ontological* type of transcendent experience reflects a desire to live and to survive as well as a struggle against death and nothingness. In one way or another, we want to survive, either biologically or spiritually—for example, in our contribution to making things better for the human race. It seems to me that this

---

4. See Roy, *Coherent Christianity*, chapter 10.

type of experience could bring about an appreciation of the mystery of humanity's collective origins, of the creative act of God, of a God who sustains us in existence and in life. This fits within the Christian vision whereby the almighty Father created us and gives us a future, out of love, in every instant, in the wisdom of his Word and in the breath of his Spirit.

The *ethical* type of transcendent experience is related to the demands of the human conscience, to its search for moral uprightness, to its natural reverence for the great values, such as respect for others, honesty, justice, love. It seems to me that this type of experience could produce an appreciation of the commitment of the prophets of yesterday and today, from Amos to Gandhi and Romero, and of Jesus himself—all of whom gave their lives for humanity's sake. From this experience could emerge the need for forgiveness—Christ the liberator's effective forgiveness, extended in acts of human forgiveness—and the need to receive the powerful breath of the Holy Spirit.

The *interpersonal* type of transcendent experience flows from a longing for a loving presence that is unfailing, incapable of abandonment or rejection. It may entail a resolve to complete faithfulness to a Presence beyond compare. In this type of experience we touch the existence of a personal Being, or perhaps more accurately, a Being that is triply personal: the Trinity. The communion of these three Persons will heighten the desire to experience otherness and exchanges, with God as well as with other human beings.

The Challenge of a Personalist Interpretation

Whatever the experiential validity of each of these four types, the danger of pantheism—an impersonal conception of the divine—is always lurking. In aesthetic experiences, it takes the form of a veneration offered to a universal spirit that pervades the cosmos (as with stoicism). In ontological experiences, there is a sense of an ineffable Being (as with Heidegger's philosophy). In ethical experiences, it takes the form of an idolatry toward a great value

The Transcendent Experience and Jesus Christ

that motivates while demanding very little (as with dictatorships, which are intended to promote justice and fraternity but instead favor power above all, or as with a certain form of republicanism, which wants to impose Western-style democracy without taking into account ethnic and cultural mindsets). In interpersonal experiences, it involves a will to own the other, either physically or psychologically, related to a love that excites while excluding the gift of self.

It is not easy to move from the notion of an anonymous divinity—claiming to be faceless on the grounds that any representation implies limits—to the names of God found in the Bible and celebrated by Pseudo-Dionysius the Areopagite.[5] It is not easy to move from an impersonal idea, principle, or spirit to the presence of a personal God who calls those who have benefited from a transcendent experience. Nevertheless, this movement to a relationship with the Trinity was carried out by the Church Fathers during the first few centuries of the Common Era. Amid the early controversies with the Gnostics, Stoics, and Platonists, they managed to lay the groundwork for the conversion of many of their contemporaries to faith in Jesus Christ.[6] The example of these patristic writers living in pre-Christian societies should be a sign of hope for us today in our efforts to evangelize our post-Christian societies.

If we wish to follow—in our own way, of course—in the footsteps of the Church Fathers, we will require creativity in the use of language, that is, a development of meanings that relate to the actual lived experiences, of which transcendent experiences are a case in point. This proposed approach will have to meet the needs of both those who have been astonished by their transcendent experiences and those Christian witnesses who must relate such experiences to biblical revelation. It will require a great deal

---

5. The Areopagite's apophatic rigor (negations) with respect to images of God does not eliminate but rather brings to completion his kataphatic praise (affirmations) of the divine names. That which is to be denied must first be affirmed.

6. The works of Justin Martyr, apologist and saint, come to mind, for example.

of versatility, as it involves finding the appropriate words and symbols to speak of these experiences in order to place them in a Judeo-Christian context.

A Question of Credibility

It is also important for us to focus on the transition from the fourth to the fifth element—that is, from discovery, with unexpressed (or barely expressed) simple intuition, to an articulated interpretation. Such a formulation inevitably develops in an interpretive framework: namely, dependent on a Christian vision of life. This formulation will often be appreciated, as it connects with a person's or group's natural desire to understand the transcendent aspect of certain moments of their life. For this reason, it can play an important role in a pre-evangelization.

That is why, going beyond relativism when it comes to many possible interpretations, I proposed a credible Christian interpretation of transcendent experiences. I believe it is credible for various reasons: in remaining close to the reality of those who have had one of these experiences, in being marked by a psychological empathy, and in opening oneself to a light coming from biblical traditions.

Let us note, in conclusion, that Jesus did not belittle the scribe's "wise answer" when he said to the man: "You are not far from the kingdom of God" (Mark 12:34).

Conclusion

The aim of this book was to draw the reader's attention to the importance of transcendent experiences, because they foster attentiveness to Mystery. It seems essential to me that, in light of the great spiritual hunger among people today, competent guides help us to recognize signs of the divine in our lives. Transcendent experiences are such signs, of a more emotional type, that find their place alongside other signs of a more interrogative and reflective nature. To define the subject of my inquiry, I have focused on experiences that, while not excluding thought, are more emotional.

In reaction to the work of William James, some theologians have taken issue with his interest in particular instances of religious experience; they claim that God may be found only in the everyday. It is true that God is no more present or at work in these instances than in the routine of ordinary life, but they provide occasions where God is "felt by the heart."[1] In other words, we do not always encounter God in the same way. A person's relationship with God can grow before or after transcendent experiences. But through such experiences, people discover a specific aspect of God, namely, *as* transcendent, infinite, Other, the fascinating and formidable Mystery. As long as this essential otherness of the Transcendent is not perceived, a person risks reducing everything to fit their own small and narrow world, closing themselves off from the unknown and missing what is essential.

1. Pascal, *Pensées*, 215.

The Feeling of Transcendence, an Experience of God?

I have therefore not said that transcendent experiences should be glorified as if the divine limited itself to them. Rather, in insisting on the need to cultivate the fruit of such experiences, I suggested that the path to religious maturity lies not in clinging to these experiences, but in growing psychically, morally, and intellectually, as well as finding ways to create the proper conditions for a mystical consciousness to emerge. The latter enables a person to see God in all things and all things in God, as well as to engage in society with a motivation and a detachment that are more respectful of nature and of human beings.

I hope that in defining the transcendent experience, analyzing its six basic elements, suggesting four main types of experiences, and offering examples and narratives, this book has given the reader an idea of the places, times, and occasions where a person can discover the most important reality there is. In discussing the views of thinkers who see these religious experiences as illusory, I have noted the limitations of these thinkers' positions. The differences in perspective boil down to two incompatible visions of the person: the human being is either confined within a whole made up of finite things, or else the human being is open, thanks to his questioning and his freedom, to the Infinite whom he or she desires and seeks.

Critiques of these experiences are more useful than rejections of them, countering the less competent gurus' tendency to misrepresent the value of transcendent experiences, to naively suggest that their results are always positive, and to ignore difficulties related to the psyche and intentionality, self-consciousness and otherness, evil and non-experience. To avoid digressions and to learn as much as possible from the sociologists, philosophers, and psychologists with whom I have chosen to dialogue, I have sometimes refrained from expressing my disagreement with some of their opinions. For me it is more important to share in the dynamic belief held by so many of them: that transcendent experiences are extremely valuable. They are an encounter with an incomparable Presence who welcomes us unconditionally and gives us a Breath beyond measure.

Conclusion

Having reached the end of this inquiry, the honest reader will ask himself: When all is said and done, what am I to think of these transcendent experiences? Are they valid and credible? Do they help me broaden my horizons and my outlook on life? Do I take the feeling of transcendence seriously enough in my own life and in the lives of others to want to allow a mystical consciousness to emerge within me? If this book helped to heighten such personal questions for the reader, it will have achieved its aim. Indeed, I wished not only to shed light on the issue of transcendent experiences, but also to assist each person in making up his or her own mind when it comes to the great Mystery who gives meaning to human life.

Bibliography

Aurobindo, Sri. *Essays on the Gita*. Pondicherry: Sri Aurobindo Ashram, 1970.
Bamberger, John. "Religion as Illusion? Freud's Challenge to Theology." *Concilium* 6.2 (1966) 38–45.
Barth, Karl. *Anselm: Fides Quaerens Intellectum*. Translated by Ian W. Robertson. London: SCM, 1960.
———. "Brunners Schleiermacherbuch." *Zwischen den Zeiten* 2.8 (1924) 49–64.
———. *Church Dogmatics*. Edited by G. W. Bromiley and T. F. Torrance. Study ed. 31 vols. Edinburgh: T. & T. Clark, 2009.
———. *The Epistle to the Romans*. Translated by Edwyn C. Hoskyns. Oxford: Oxford University Press, 1933.
———. *Protestant Theology in the Nineteenth Century: Its Background and History*. Translated by Brian Cozens and John Bowden. London: SCM, 1972.
Barzel, Bernard. *Mystique de l'Ineffable dans l'hindouisme et le christianisme. Çankara et Eckhart*. Paris: Cerf, 1982.
Benz, Ernst. *The Mystical Sources of German Romantic Philosophy*. Translated by Blair R. Reynolds and Eunice M. Paul. Allison Park, PA: Pickwick, 1983.
Berger, Peter L. *A Rumor of Angels: Modern Society and the Rediscovery of the Supernatural*. Garden City, NY: Doubleday, 1969.
The Bhagavad-Gita. Translated by Robert C. Zaehner. London: Clarendon, 1969.
Bibby, Reginald W. *Canada's Teens: Today, Yesterday, and Tomorrow*. Toronto: Stoddart, 2001.
———. *Restless Gods: The Renaissance of Religion in Canada*. Toronto: Stoddart, 2002.
Bourdeau, Gilles. "Jean Mouroux : l'actualité de l'expérientiel." *Le Supplément* 104 (1973) 3–25.
Brunner, Emil. *Die Mystik und das Wort*. 2nd rev ed. Tübingen: Mohr, 1928.
Bucke, Richard Maurice. *Cosmic Consciousness: A Study in the Evolution of the Human Mind*. New York: E. P. Dutton, 1969.

Bibliography

Bultmann, Rudolph. *Existence and Faith: Shorter Writings of Rudolph Bultmann.* Translated by Schubert M. Ogden. London: Collins, 1964.

Burke, Edmund. *A Philosophical Enquiry into the Origin of Our Ideas of the Sublime and Beautiful.* Oxford: Oxford University Press, 2008.

Clark, Walter Houston. "Mysticism as a Basic Concept in Defining the Religious Self." In *From Religious Experience to a Religious Attitude*, edited by André Godin. Studies in Religious Psychology. Brussels: Lumen Vitae, 1964.

Collins, Alice. "Barth's Relationship to Schleiermacher: A Reassessment." *Studies in Religion/Sciences religieuses* 17.2 (1988) 213–24.

Crookall, Robert. *The Interpretation of Cosmic and Mystical Experiences.* Cambridge: James Clarke, 1969.

Dalbiez, Roland. *Psychoanalytical Method and the Doctrine of Freud.* Translated by T. F. Lindsay. 2 vols. London: Longmans, Green, 1941.

de Muralt, André. *The Idea of Phenomenology: Husserlian Exemplarism.* Translated by Garry L. Breckon. Northwestern University Studies in Phenomenology & Existential Philosophy. Edited by James M. Edie. Evanston, IL: Northwestern University Press, 1974.

Delbrêl, Madeleine. *We, the Ordinary People of the Streets.* Translated by David Louis Schindler Jr. and Charles F. Mann. Grand Rapids, MI: Eerdmans, 2000.

Dempsey, Peter. *Freud, Psychoanalysis, Catholicism.* Cork: Mercier, 1956.

Dhavamony, Mariasusai. *Hindouisme et foi chrétienne.* Montreal: Bellarmin, 1993.

Dufrenne, Mikel. *The Phenomenology of Aesthetic Experience.* Translated by Edward S. Casey et al. Evanston, IL: Northwestern University Press, 1973.

Elkin, Henry. "On the Origin of the Self." *Psychoanalysis and the Psychoanalytical Review* 45.4 (1958–59) 57–76.

Evans-Pritchard, E. E. *Theories of Primitive Religion.* Oxford: Clarendon, 1966.

Feuerbach, Ludwig. *Sämtliche Werke.* Vol. 1. Leipzig: Otto Wigand, 1846–1888.

Freud, Sigmund. "Civilization and Its Discontents." In *The Standard Edition of the Complete Psychological Works of Sigmund Freud*, edited and translated by James Strachey, 64–145. London: Hogarth, 1961.

———. "The Future of an Illusion." In *The Standard Edition of the Complete Psychological Works of Sigmund Freud*, edited and translated by James Strachey, 5–56. London: Hogarth, 1961.

———. "Leonardo da Vinci and a Memory of His Childhood." In *The Standard Edition of the Complete Psychological Works of Sigmund Freud*, edited and translated by James Strachey, 63–137. London: Hogarth, 1957.

———. "Totem and Taboo." In *The Standard Edition of the Complete Psychological Works of Sigmund Freud*, edited and translated by James Strachey, 1–161. London: Hogarth, 1961.

Fromm, Erich. *The Art of Loving.* New York: HarperPerennial, 2000.

———. *The Dogma of Christ and Other Essays on Religion, Psychology and Culture.* Translated by James Luther Adams. New York: Holt, 1992.

Bibliography

———. *Psychoanalysis and Religion*. New Haven, CT: Yale University Press, 1950.

———. "Some Post-Marxian and Post-Freudian Thoughts on Religion and Religiousness." *Concilium* 6.8 (1972) 146–54.

Girard, René. *Deceit, Desire, and the Novel: Self and Other in Literary Structure*. Translated by Yvonne Freccero. Baltimore: Johns Hopkins, 1965.

Godin, André. *The Psychological Dynamics of Religious Experience*. Translated by Mary Turton. Birmingham, AL: Religion Education, 1985.

Goettman, Alphonse. *Dialogue on the Path of Initiation: An Introduction to the Life and Thought of Karlfried Graf Dürckheim*. Translated by Theodore Nottingham and Rebecca Nottingham. New York: Globe, 1991.

Goritcheva, Tatiana. *Nous, convertis d'Union soviétique*. Paris: Nouvelle Cité, 1983.

Grand'Maison, Jacques, et al., eds. *Le défi des générations. Enjeux sociaux et religieux du Québec d'aujourd'hui*, Cahiers d'études pastorale 15. Montreal: Fides, 1995.

Grand'Maison, Jacques, and Solange Lefebvre, eds. *Une génération bouc émissaire. Enquête sur les baby-boomers*, Cahiers d'études pastorales 12. Montreal: Fides, 1993.

Greeley, Andrew M. *The Sociology of the Paranormal: A Reconnaissance*. Studies in Religion and Ethnicity, Sage Research Papers in the Social Sciences 3. Beverly Hills: Sage, 1975.

Green, Julian. *Then Shall the Dust Return*. Translated by James Whitall. New York: Harper & Brothers, 1941.

Hardy, Alister. *The Spiritual Nature of Man: A Study of Contemporary Religious Experience*. Oxford: Clarendon, 1979.

Hay, David. *Exploring Inner Space: Scientists and Religious Experience*. London: Mowbray, 1987.

Heaney, John J. *The Sacred and the Psychic: Parapsychology and Christian Theology*. New York: Paulist, 1984.

Heidegger, Martin. *Pathmarks*. Cambridge: Cambridge University Press, 1999.

Hesse, Hermann. *Siddhartha*. Translated by Hilda Rosner. New York: New Directions, 1970.

Jacob, Edmond. *Theology of the Old Testament*. Translated by Arthur W. Heathcote and Philip J. Allcock. London: Hodder & Stoughton, 1958.

James, William. *Varieties of Religious Experience: A Study in Human Nature*. Centenary ed. New York: Routledge, 2002.

Johnston, William. *Silent Music: The Science of Meditation*. New York: Harper & Row, 1974.

Jones, Ernest. *The Last Phase 1919–1939. Sigmund Freud: Life and Work*. Vol. 3, London: Hogarth, 1957.

Kant, Immanuel. *Critique of the Power of Judgment*. Translated by Paul Guyer and Eric Matthews. Cambridge: Cambridge University Press, 2001.

———. *Observations on the Feeling of the Beautiful and Sublime and Other Writings*. Cambridge Texts in the History of Philosophy. Edited by Karl

Bibliography

Ameriks and Desmond M. Clarke. Cambridge: Cambridge University Press, 2011.
Kellenberger, J. "Mysticism and Drugs." *Religious Studies* 14.2 (1978) 175–91.
Klein, Melanie, and Joan Riviere. *Love, Hate and Reparation.* New York: Norton, 1964.
Koestler, Arthur. *Drinkers of Infinity: Essays 1955–1967.* London: Hutchinson, 1968.
Kris, Ernst. *Psychoanalytic Explorations in Art.* New York: International Universities Press, 1952.
Küng, Hans. *Does God Exist? An Answer for Today.* Translated by Edward Quinn. Garden City, NY: Doubleday, 1980.
Lacelle, Elisabeth J. "Karl Barth: Un théologien de la parole prophétique dans l'Église et dans la société." *Studies in Religion/Sciences religieuses* 7.2 (1978) 137–47.
———. "Pour une épistémologie de la relation. L'expérience comme lieu relationnel poiétique en théologie." In *L'Expérience comme lieu théologique*, edited by Elisabeth J. Lacelle and Thomas R. Potvin. Héritage et projet, 47–73. Montreal: Fides, 1983.
Laski, Marghanita. *Ecstasy: A Study of Some Secular and Religious Experiences.* New York: Greenwood, 1968.
Lebeaux, Yves. "Les critiques psychanalytiques de la religion." In *Initiation à la pratique de la théologie*, edited by Bernard Lauret and François Refoulé, 493–507. Paris: Cerf, 1982.
Leuba, Jean-Louis. *Études barthiennes.* Geneva: Labor et Fides, 1986.
Lonergan, Bernard. *Method in Theology.* Collected Works of Bernard Lonergan. Edited by Robert M. Doran and John D. Dadosky. Vol. 14. Toronto: University of Toronto Press, 2017.
Longinus. *On Sublimity.* Translated by D. A. Russel. Oxford: Clarendon, 1965.
Mahler, Margaret S., et al. *The Psychological Birth of the Human Infant: Symbiosis and Individuation.* New York: Basic Books, 1975.
Margolis, Robert D., and Kirk W. Elifson. "A Typology of Religious Experience." *Journal for the Scientific Study of Religion* 18.1 (1979) 61–67.
Maritain, Jacques. *Approaches to God.* Translated by Peter O'Reilly. World Perspectives. Edited by Ruth Nanda Anshen. New York: Harper, 1954.
———. *The Peasant of the Garonne: An Old Layman Questions Himself about the Present Time.* Translated by Michael Cuddihy and Elizabeth Hughes. New York: Holt, Rinehart and Winston, 1968.
Maslow, Abraham H. *Religions, Values, and Peak-Experiences.* New York: Viking, 1970.
———. *Toward a Psychology of Being.* 3rd ed. New York: Wiley, 1999.
May, Rollo. *The Courage to Create.* New York: Norton, 1975.
Miquel, Pierre. *Le Vocabulaire latin de l'expérience spirituelle dans la tradition monastique et canoniale de 1050 à 1250.* Théologie historique 79. Paris: Beauchesne, 1989.

Bibliography

Moody, Raymond A. *Life after Life: The Investigation of a Phenomenon—Survival of Bodily Death*. St Simons Island, GA: Mockingbird, 1975.

———. *Reflections on Life after Life*. New York: Bantam, 1978.

Niebuhr, Reinhold. *The Nature and Destiny of Man: A Christian Interpretation*. 2 vols. London: Nisbet, 1941.

Ortigues, Marie-Cécile, and Edmond Ortigues. *Oedipe africain*. Paris: Plon, 1966.

Otto, Rudolf. *The Idea of the Holy: An Inquiry into the Non-Rational Factor in the Idea of the Divine and Its Relation to the Rational*. Translated by John W. Harvey. New York: Oxford University Press, 1958.

———. *Mysticism East and West: A Comparative Analysis of the Nature of Mysticism*. Translated by Bertha L. Bracey and Richenda C. Payne. New York: Meridian, 1957.

Panikkar, Raimundo. *The Trinity and the Religious Experience of Man: Icon—Person—Mystery*. Maryknoll, NY: Orbis, 1973.

Pascal, Blaise. *Pensées*. Translated and edited by Roger Ariew. Indianapolis: Hackett, 2005.

Pelletier, Pierre. *Les Dieux que nous sommes. Le Mouvement du potentiel humain*. Montreal: Fides, 1992.

Plé, Albert. *Freud et la religion*. Paris: Cerf, 1968.

Ricoeur, Paul. *Freud and Philosophy: An Essay on Interpretation*. New Haven, CT: Yale University Press, 1970.

Roy, Louis. "Arnaud Desjardins et le christianisme (1ère partie)." *Nouveau dialogue* 94 (1993) 16–22.

———. "Arnaud Desjardins et le christianisme (2ème partie)." *Nouveau dialogue* 95 (1993) 9–14.

———. *Coherent Christianity: Toward an Articulate Faith*. Eugene, OR: Wipf and Stock, 2018.

———. "Expériences de transcendance et conversion." *La vie spirituelle* 80 (2000) 459–69.

———. "Inclusive Language Regarding God." *Worship* 65.3 (1991) 207–15.

———. *Transcendent Experiences: Phenomenology and Critique*. Toronto: University of Toronto Press, 2001.

Sagne, Jean-Claude. "De l'illusion au symbole, la reconnaissance du père." *Lumière et vie* 20.104 (1971) 38–58.

Sartre, Jean-Paul. *Nausea*. New York: New Directions, 2013.

Schleiermacher, Friedrich. *Christian Faith: A New Translation and Critical Edition*. Translated by Terrence N. Tice et al. Edited by Catherine L. Kelsey and Terrence N. Tice. 2 vols. Louisville: Westminster John Knox, 2016.

———. *On Religion: Speeches to Its Cultured Despisers*. Translated by John Oman. Louisville: Westminster John Knox, 1994.

Schüssler Fiorenza, Francis. "The Responses of Barth and Ritschl to Feuerbach." *Studies in Religion/Sciences religieuses* 7.2 (1978) 149–66.

Skinner, Martin M. "Musique et paroles sacrées." *Communauté Chrétienne* 24.144 (1985) 556–65.

Bibliography

Stace, Walter T. *Mysticism and Philosophy*. London: MacMillan, 1961.
Standal, Stanley W., and Raymond J. Corsini, eds. *Critical Incidents in Psychotherapy*. Englewood Cliffs, NJ: Prentice-Hall, 1959.
Strauss, Leo. *Spinoza's Critique of Religion*. New York: Schocken, 1965.
Tillich, Paul. *The Courage to Be*. London: Collins, 1967.
Valla, Jean-Pierre. *Les états étranges de la conscience*. Paris: Presses Universitaires de France, 1992.
Vergote, Antoine. *Guilt and Desire: Religious Attitudes and Their Pathological Derivatives*. Translated by M. H. Wood. New Haven, CT: Yale University Press, 1988.
———. *The Religious Man: A Psychological Study of Religious Attitudes*. Translated by Marie-Bernard Said. Dublin: Gill and MacMillan, 1969.
Vernette, Jean. *Réincarnation, résurrection, communiquer avec l'au-delà. Les mystères de la Vie après la vie*. Mulhouse, France: Salvator, 1988.
von Dürckheim, Karlfried Graf. *Our Two-fold Origin: As Promise, Experience and Mission*. Translated by George Unwin. London: George Allen & Unwin, 1983.
Weil, Simone. *Waiting on God*. Translated by Emma Craufurd. London: Routledge and Kegan Paul, 1951.
Welte, Bernhard. *Das Licht des Nichts: Von der Möglichkeit neuer religiöser Erhfahrung*. Düsseldorf: Patmos Verlag, 1980.
Xhaufflaire, Marcel. *Feuerbach et la théologie de la sécularisation*. Paris: Cerf, 1970.
Zaehner, Robert C. *Mysticism Sacred and Profane: An Inquiry into Some Varieties of Praeternatural Experience*. Oxford: Clarendon, 1957.
Zielinski, Wladimir. "Une nouvelle génération de croyants." *Les Quatre Fleuves* 14 (1981) 69–123.
Zilboorg, Gregory. *Psychoanalysis and Religion*. New York: Farrar, Straus and Cudahy, 1962.

www.ingramcontent.com/pod-product-compliance
Lightning Source LLC
Chambersburg PA
CBHW070924160426
43193CB00011B/1574